GET UP WITH FLEAS

A MEMOIR OF ABUSE AND GRATITUDE

ALEXANDER GAMBON

CONTENTS

1

WRITTEN BY THE VICTOR

Everyone thinks their own life story is interesting, don't they? They rarely are. But still, I feel compelled to write this down. I am 33 years old, so I can only hope that this is not my *entire* life story. This is a memoir of my life's most significant and formative events so far, merely as remembered by me at this moment. First, though, I want to explain why I am writing this. Why is it at all interesting or important to write down my recollection of my past?

I am writing this for future generations to have. I have been thinking a lot about how the stories I hear from my mother, grandfather, or aunts and uncles don't all fit together. There is much mystery surrounding what happened in the hidden moments of prior generations. The way my mother was parented, for example, directly influenced the person she became, the childhood she gave me, and therefore who I am today. As I try to connect the dots between my history and their history, some things will never make sense. So, for future interested generations, I want to leave this as an attempt to explain where I've come from. My children should understand the legacy they inherit, and the cycles they are breaking.

I am also writing this for myself. I think a lot about the past. I reflect on my mindset, attitudes, identity, and how they have evolved over the years. I think about my history and where I've come from more than is probably necessary, and perhaps if I write it all down, I can stop thinking about it so much. I've found the practice of writing-down to be very useful in smaller areas of my life. I tend to ruminate and obsess over the process of merely remembering important information. There is something in my brain that is telling me that if I stop thinking about something for a moment, it will vanish forever – perhaps a vestige of OCD that has been nurtured by trauma. So, I turn to note-taking, journaling, arrays of documents, and second-brain models to give my looping mind some relief from having to hold everything in my mind's eye at all times. Now, I want to apply that method to my entire history. I will write it all down. It will always be in the book if I need to read it again.

But in order to understand what this memoir truly is, I need to set forth what it is definitely not.

This is not anyone else's story. Like anyone, my life intersects with others and I am enmeshed with other people in inextricable ways. Even still, I will avoid telling other people's stories, except those that are also my own. I only mention siblings by name if they have explicitly agreed to be named here. This is not the stage for theorizing on how our childhood affected my siblings, or even trying to tell my wife's stories for her – except insofar as I have been affected by the people I discuss. These are my stories, how I remember them.

This is not fully accurate. Not all of these stories expose every single detail of the situations discussed. It is a set of writings limited by my own memory. Every story should be inferred as merely being my recollection, and not necessarily imbued with any historical accuracy. This is how I happen to remember these stories at my current age of 33. If I were writing this at 22 or perhaps 44, I would certainly remember them differently. Memories are inherently fictions.

This is not a chronological timeline. My life is presented as I remember it – not in sequential order, but in parallel strands. Each memory connects to the next not by just the passage of time, but by the feeling it carries. School, home, work, marriage – each a thread of stories from a larger fabric. Many chapters are vast swaths of time, from a single lens: only to go back in time in the next chapter, and tell it from another perspective.

This doesn't reflect the totality of my life. This isn't and can't be a totally holistic encyclopedia of everything I've experienced. I'm sure I will tell many stories to my children that are not in this book, and there are many stories that I've already forgotten. As a memoir, this is a collection of stories, but it is not an autobiography. There are certain foundational and formative events that I want to record for posterity, and it happens to be the case that many formative events were traumatic events. Just because that is much of what is in this book, certainly doesn't mean that is the entirety of my lived experience.

So, again, what is this book?

This is a history book, written by the victor. Life is messy, and memories don't always make sense, or connect neatly together. Still, everything presented here was formative for me. I am sharing this publicly not in the expectation that my story will be meaningful to every other stranger, but because the very act of publishing it allows me to claim who I am: I am this story.

It is a charted course from adversity to fatherhood. It is my journey through deconstruction into reconstruction. It is a reflection on mental health and trauma. It is a record of the three different names I've borne. It is the three times I've stolen something, the three times I've flown into a violent rage, and the three times I've made a stupidly huge gamble that somehow *didn't* end in disaster. And most certainly, it is the ramblings of a silly man.

2

A CONVENIENT LIE

M y mother, in her youth, was what one might call a wayward soul. She was brilliant, deeply sensitive, and often searched for something to anchor herself to. She had two older brothers and one younger sister, and they were raised in the Catholic Church. The stories I've heard of their own childhoods are murky. Their parents were, by all reports, deeply complex. Their father was an attentive and ever-present provider – he also drank heavily for a few years, withheld affection, and had a nasty temper. Their mother was creative, bubbly, and wrote marvelous stories of fantastic creatures – she also battled suicidality and depression, and was hospitalized multiple times.

Each of my mother's siblings became engineers, like their father. My mother was more sensitive, more empathic. She obtained a master's degree in speech language pathology, and would later work in the hospital system doing speech therapy.

One night in January of 1990, she was at the Georgia Square Mall in Athens, Georgia. She met a man who was operating a magazine kiosk. He was a transient, working odd jobs and hawking magazines across the country. She was 24 years old, finishing up college, and was looking for a risk to take. After some flirting, they attended a party together, and he invited her back to a hotel room in Atlanta. In what would become a rather pivotal moment in my life, she became pregnant.

After that night, they didn't speak for a while. Not until two months later, when the Georgia Division of Family and Children Services sent the man a letter informing him of her pregnancy. He called her on the phone. What follows is a transcript of the call that my mother wrote down at the time.

"You're pregnant? I'm in shock."

"Yes, I'm pregnant," she said. "You're the father."

"Yeah I know I am. You're not gonna get an abortion right?"

"No," she said. "I'm not getting an abortion."

"Good. I hate abortions," the man replied. "Do you have a job? Any money?"

"Not right now," she said.

"Do you need me to send you money? For baby stuff?"

"That would be nice," the woman replied. "You have my home address. I'm enrolling in Medicaid to help pay for things too. I've been told that child support is not determined until after the birth. It could be determined in a court, but if you come forward and work with me on it, it will be a lot easier."

The man thought for a moment. "You got my address?"

"I only have your work address."

"Yeah, that's my mailing address right now. Send me a letter with what you think you need."

"You write me first," the woman said, flatly. "You have my contact info if you actually want to be part of this."

"You better let me see my baby," the man said.

She replied, "I'll let you see your baby."

After that conversation, she never heard from him again. That man had no interest in being a father. He threw away her contact information and left the state.

My mother's siblings attended Georgia Tech, and were involved in the Catholic center on campus. That community rallied around my mother, and supported her. They threw her a baby shower, and gave her encouragement.

I was born in the fall of 1990, in Atlanta, as Alexander Martin Leonard Gambon – the first of three names I'd eventually bear. 'Leonard' came from a family friend of my grandparents who passed away around the same time I was born. (Incidentally, we are distantly related to Michael Gambon, esteemed Irish actor.)

My mother was finishing school and working as a single parent, so I spent a lot of time with my grandparents, and the Gorslines. The Gorslines were a family from church that my mother and her parents knew. I was named Alexander after Alexander Gorsline, the father of that family. They had three children in middle or high school, and they took care of me almost every day for three years. We took walks in the neighborhood, I played in their tree fort, and snuggled up with them like they were my own family. The precious few videos of me when I was very young were filmed by the Gorslines, as they cared for me. In many ways, they imprinted upon me what a loving family looked like – a reference point that would be vital in the years to come.

However, even the best influences can't prevent the curiosity and missteps of childhood, and like all children, I probed for consequences to my actions, looking for things to get away with.

I have only physically stolen something three times in my life. The first, when I was three, out of curiosity. The second, when I was 10, out of jealousy. The third time, when I was 15, out of bitterness.

For that first occasion of theft, when I was three, I was with my mother on a weekend, shopping at Food Lion. In the checkout lane, I spotted a rack of hot wheels cars. I took one, and smuggled it into my pocket, mentally contriving a lie to tell. When we got to the car, I had the toy in my hand.

"Where did you get that?" my mom asked.

"The lady at the checkout saw me looking at it, and she told me I could have it!" I lied.

"Oh, that's nice," my mom said.

My mother should not have believed that. Even at such a young age, my mind started clicking away, trying to understand why she allowed this to transpire. She should have questioned such an obvious falsehood, and known that cashiers don't just hand out toys. Even though I was the one who had lied, and created a deception, I lost some trust in my mom that day. In that moment, she readily accepted a convenient lie instead of searching for the truth. The reality she lived in was flexible, willing to morph itself into the most comfortable shape. I didn't conceive of that consciously, but I went home disappointed.

3

BREEDING RESENTMENT

My mother married a man when I was three. He was a short, burly man with his own wayward childhood defined by death, drugs, and mental illness. But the man she met in the church seemed to have it all together. He was charismatic, and direct. He poured concrete for a living, working for a friend who owned a construction company. He seemed to be the strong protector sort, and told her he would keep her safe.

She quickly got pregnant, and they bought a tiny house in a small town called Flowery Branch. The house had three small bedrooms, and one bathroom. The kitchen and living room weren't much more than a hallway. Oddly, a grotesque stone creature hung just outside the front door – some sort of gargoyle or goblin. My mother theorized that the prior homeowners "must have been Buddhists." The front yard had a massive oak tree that towered over the house, and a short gravel driveway. A blue, metal gate that just barely spanned the driveway offered a false security from would-be burglars, as any car could easily just drive around it.

The property had a half-acre hilly backyard, and the decaying fence around the back half did nothing to stop the occasional cow from roaming into our yard. We were on well water, pumped out of the natural water table, and the well pump broke down constantly.

The town at the time was a dusty collection of dirt roads and wooded farmland. Atlanta was an hour to the southwest, and it would be many years before the urban sprawl expanded to where we lived. The local economy consisted of a gas station and a man who sold bootleg VHS tapes out of his trunk. We would spend lots of our time traveling to Gainesville, the town north of us, for church and groceries.

My mother's new husband adopted me legally. In the adoption process, they worked with an attorney who advised them to send a letter to my biological father asking him to voluntarily waive his rights. They didn't know if they even had the correct address for him, and got no response. The paperwork was completed, and they dropped my second middle name, Leonard, and replaced my last name with my new father's.

My earliest memories with my new father were warm. He was always just "dad" to me. I had a signature song that he would clap along with. "Bip bip bip, bop-ah wah-wah," I'd sing. He nicknamed me "Little Bipper" and he emblazoned that moniker on my carseat in permanent ink. I felt very bonded to him, and wanted his affection more than anything.

But the early signs of problems were there. He drank too much alcohol. He didn't tolerate disagreement. He forced our mom to quit her well-paying job as a speech therapist to be a traditional, stay-at-home mom, fully reliant on his small and inconsistent income.

My mother looked for purpose where she could, but didn't know where to find it. She attached herself to an endless carousel of holistic healing remedies, chiropractors, herbal supplements, and pyramid schemes that whittled away whatever of the family's finances weren't already stolen by our dad's drinking.

They quickly had more children. My mother was pregnant for nearly my entire child-hood, each coming one after the other. Our dad's alcoholism worsened, our mom's denial deepened, and violence coursed through our family like shockwaves.

The first of my siblings was born when I was three, and the last when I was 12. In total she had six children after me – two boys, a girl, a boy, and then two girls. We were crammed on top of each other, in a tiny house in a tiny town. The family grew, but the house did not.

4

UPHILL BOTH WAYS

My memories are sparse and few from my early childhood, but I remember the day I got my first pair of glasses. I was three years old, and the optometrist handed me a pair of wiry red frames. As I slipped them on, the world around me suddenly came into sharp focus. That same year, I learned to read, spurred on by my incessant curiosity about road signs. "Mommy, what does that say?" I would ask, pointing at every passing billboard and stop sign. At home, my mom used a book called "Teach Your Child to Read in 100 Easy Lessons." I breezed through half of the lessons and soon found myself reading fluently.

The librarians at the local library soon came to know me by name. I was the precocious three year old handing them stacks of chapter books, and returning them fully read just days later. If anything was magic, it was that library. It was a portal, each visit unlocking a new world.

In Kindergarten, I was the only child awake during naptime. I strategically positioned my nap mat by the window so that I could read my chapter books while the other children slept.

Soon after Kindergarten started, I went to the school library for the first time. It was smaller than the local library, but I was excited. Books on demand, right there at school. As I walked through the aisles of books, I realized something was different about how these were laid out. Instead of being sorted by genre or author, they were sorted by grade level. The large "K" hung over a section of board books, reserved specifically for the Kindergartners. These books were simple, and I knew they would be boring.

I paused for a moment, looking over towards the section labeled "3rd Grade." Hesitantly, I looked around, wondering if I would be scolded or punished for venturing into sections not meant for me.

No one was watching. I slunk over to the aisles of chapter books, and my eyes landed on a book titled *Mrs. Piggle-Wiggle*. *Mrs. Piggle-Wiggle* would become a favorite of mine – a whimsical story about a witchy woman who cared for all the kids in the neighborhood whose parents had given up on them. She taught them virtue, kindness, and self-acceptance, in spite of their parents who had thrown their hands up and labeled their kids as beyond help.

I wound my way around the school library, clutching the book. I headed towards the librarian's desk, intentionally walking past the Kindergarten section, hoping it looked like I had just come from there. I offered the librarian the book.

The librarian peered at me over her glasses, taking the book. She smirked, and said, "Don't you think you should get something a bit smaller?"

I shook my head. "No, I want this one."

"Okay," she said. "You can bring it back tomorrow if you want a different book instead."

I breathed a sigh of relief. I hadn't gotten caught.

The next day, I brought the book back. The librarian smiled. "Was it a bit too difficult? Need one more your size?"

"No," I shook my head, "I finished it." I logged the book in the "Accelerated Reader" program – a school-wide competition to read the most books and earn prizes. I watched as my points increased. Reading was the only thing I wanted to do, and earning points felt good – proof of my literary conquests.

After three months of Kindergarten, the school moved me to first grade. In an effort to make sure I was "challenged," they also had me spend half the day with the second graders. Well, I was certainly challenged. Not academically, but socially. I spent half the day with children more than a year older than me, and half the day with children more than two years older than me, and never enough time to bond with anyone. I was very isolated and alone, and all I had were my books.

At the end of first grade, the results of the Accelerated Reader competition were posted in the library. First by grade, and then the top 20 students in the school, overall. I looked at the list. At the bottom were some third graders, followed by a mixture of fourth and fifth graders. Then, at the top, was me. I was the number-one scorer in the reading program across the entire school, out-scoring even the fifth graders.

I wondered if I should feel a sense of pride, but instead I felt confused. I didn't understand why people so much older than me weren't reading as much as me.

My social issues were worsening. I was acting out, making rude noises, and generally pleading for attention with the most obnoxious methods I could devise. My mom's solution to address this was to isolate me further, and she decided to homeschool me for second grade.

The one social outlet I had was gymnastics. One of my mom's brothers was a weightlifter who married an all-star swimmer, and their son was in gymnastics. Following their example, my mom did the same for me. I recall that the program was mostly run by young women – perhaps high school girls. We were all very young kids, and the program itself was highly gendered. The boys had to do the high bar, while the girls had to do the balance beam. I was an awkward, unathletic kid, and the high bar jump scared me. I hated having to run, leap, and grab that bar in midair, and then fall. I thought that the gender split was pointless, and I'd often ask, "can I do the balance beam instead?" The instructors made fun of me every day after that. They'd call me a girly boy, and ask me if I wanted to be a girl. I didn't. I just wanted to walk on a balance beam.

After a year of homeschool, it became clear that I needed better social adjustment. My mom sent me to public school for third grade, and my teacher was Mrs. Hoffmann. She was attentive, caring, and patient. She took the time to address me by name, and she was intentional about making sure I was engaged even when I had finished assignments far ahead of everyone else. She was my real-life Mrs. Piggle-Wiggle. Mrs. Hoffmann quickly became my idol, and I loved going to school every day. She was the first adult in my life, after the Gorslines from my earliest years, who ensured that I was not just achieving, but cared for. I resolved that when I grew up, I wanted nothing more than to be a third grade teacher.

Fourth grade was not quite as special. I missed Mrs. Hoffmann, and my social adjustment wasn't exactly on track. I would excel in my school work, but I'd also try rudely to be friends with other kids who didn't want the intrusion. I recall going up to a girl in my class one day, as we assembled at the door to head to the cafeteria.

"Do you know how to spell Mississippi?" she asked.

I stuck out my tongue and spit loudly and wetly in her face.

She shrieked. The teacher scolded me, and I was separated from the class for lunch, forced to sit at a table by myself. I didn't understand anything that had happened in that interaction. I didn't understand why the girl asked me to spell a state. *What's interesting about that?* I thought. The spitting was far more interesting to me. It was loud, it was wet, it was silly. *It should have made her laugh. Why didn't she like it?* I also didn't understand why the teacher punished me. *Didn't the teacher understand that I was trying to be friends?*

At one point, the Pokémon fad had taken the school by storm, and students were excitedly bringing in their card collections and trading them. I saw the attention they got when they showed them off – rare and precious artifacts of a home where gifts freely flowed. Anyone who had rare cards was the hero of the day, and everyone wanted to talk to them.

Then, I stole something for the second time.

A classmate put their latest pack of cards into the front pouch of their backpack. They had new cards every week. It seemed unfair, and I convinced myself that stealing his cards would merely be an act of justice.

I snuck over to his backpack during a break, and fished around for the cards. I was caught within moments, and sheepishly returned the cards and apologized.

I recall seeing the friendships and bonds that other students had, and yearning for that. I saw that generally, boys would be content playing solo – digging a hole, building some legos, or climbing a tower. Girls would move in packs, always together, always in community. I thought to myself, *I might like to be a girl, if it meant I could have friends.* My desire for approval and connection went unfulfilled.

Meanwhile, abuse at home was deepening, and my mom was sinking further into fundamentalism. She believed every story that a fear-mongering tabloid or TV channel told her, and developed a belief that middle school was not just an awkward cesspool of hormones and preteens, but Satan's playground. She believed that the devil used middle school to turn children into demons, and corrupt their souls. The bright, if somewhat unstable young woman she once was evolved into a fearful mother who clutched her children tightly without ever looking at them.

She elected to homeschool all of her children for the next three years, and I spent fifth, sixth, and seventh grade inside a private cult. I took three years of piano lessons from a neighbor, and three years of Latin lessons from our homeschool group at church – and I remember very little of either now. The only people I knew or spoke to were our family, that piano teacher, and the three other families in the homeschool group. And the emotional and physical violence got worse.

5

BETWEEN THE DEVIL AND THE DEEP BLUE SEA

Now we get to the core of it all. The salted wound, the chronic trauma. The abuse and shattering violence that permeated my childhood. Rather than spreading it out over the course of the book, let's get it all out of the way at once, shall we?

Our dad had two dogs that he brought with him from before the marriage. They were two English Bulldogs, nearly identical in appearance but polar opposite in personality. Sebastian, nicknamed Bass, was the inside dog: cuddly, warm, and tolerant. Buttons was the outside dog: defensive, snapping, and aggressive. Bass would hop up on my bed to protect me at night, and I'd burrow my toes under him to keep warm. Fleas would infest my bedsheets, but I didn't mind, as I was happy that the dog liked me. I once tried to pet Buttons, and she bit me in the stomach, leaving a scar.

I often thought that the two dogs were a lot like the two sides of my dad.

Our dad was drunk frequently, and his drunkenness was never consistent. Sometimes he would be cold and aloof while sober, and then after a few beers would be sentimental and go on long monologues. Other times, a few beers was all that was needed to unlock an angry violence. He always had an open beer when driving, and would rant about how he was a "better driver drunk than your mother is sober."

He would scream at us about how we didn't deserve anything. We didn't deserve dinner, and we didn't deserve a home. Any attempt at closeness was thwarted with a hostile insult and bullying from parent to child.

My dad would tell me repeatedly "you're not my real son." When I was young, I didn't understand this. I knew that I had a biological father somewhere out there, and that my mom's husband adopted me, but he was my *dad*. But, he made sure I knew I didn't belong.

I got the most of the physical abuse. Of course, all of us kids were hit. There was a massive wooden paddle hung on the wall, with large holes drilled through it to make it more "aerodynamic." It came off the wall frequently, and we would be hit not on our butt, but our back, as we "didn't deserve the cushion." He took a sick pleasure in enacting violence on his children.

My dad would hit me, backhand me, and then tell me I was lucky I wasn't dead. He would frequently pick me up, and throw me through the walls of our house. I would crash through drywall and end up in another room, head spinning. Then, the whole family would be told that I was responsible for the dearth of food or lack of necessities in the home, because they had to spend the money instead on repairing the walls. Sometimes they didn't repair the walls, though. They left them as a reminder of what happened if you weren't perfect.

He'd also take me outside, away from anyone who could see, and we'd go behind the van. There, he'd grab my head, and slam it over and over into the side of the van, until it left a dent.

He'd keep going, again and again. "Is this what I have to do to knock some sense into your head, you piece of shit? You should be grateful I don't fuckin' kill you."

Then he'd make me apologize for denting the family car – just another way I was ruining the family. He'd tell me "I don't care if I go to prison, if it means you finally learn a lesson."

I went inside after one of these hidden moments of violence, and confronted my mother in the kitchen.

"Do you know what he did to me?"

She just looked at me for a moment, not wanting to encourage my next sentence.

"He grabbed me by the head and slammed me into the van. He told me I was a piece of shit!"

She stirred the pot on the stove, agitated. Her body was tense and jittery, as if reckoning an internal conflict.

"Don't you think that's not okay? Is that how a dad is supposed to treat their kids?"

She turned to me with a glassy stare, all anxiety suddenly dissipated. "No, I'm sure that didn't happen," she said, matter-of-factly.

She turned back to the stove and kept cooking. This was a purity of denial I could not comprehend – still choosing a convenient lie to avoid confronting reality. I attempted this confrontation many more times, and each time ended the same way. I pushed the hurt and betrayal down, somewhere deep. Instead, I regarded it like a puzzle. My mother was a Rubik's cube to solve, and if I could just get all her pieces lined up correctly, she would save me.

When the abuse happened right in front of her, she'd get agitated and start self-harming. She'd pull the skin off her arms, or slam her head into the wall repeating the mantra "I'm a terrible mother. I'm a terrible mother. I'm a terrible mother." Simultaneously, she'd make excuses for our dad, offering various explanations to hand-wave the violence away. "He had a stressful day at work," she'd explain. Or, "That's nothing compared to what he grew up with."

We would endure the beatings, and then turn toward our mother to comfort her, and assure her she was a good mom.

The abuse was widespread, but tailored for each child. We lived together, crammed on top of each other in a tiny house, but our histories are dramatically different. Each child was forced into a toxic family system role. I was the scapegoat. There was a golden child, a mediator, a lost child. Our parents created a system that required us to turn on each other and compete. We competed for food, for attention, for love. We were taught that we were supposed to be grateful for the essentials, and they were taken away at a whim, or doled out unequally. Dinner withheld, locked out of the house, or beaten for asking questions.

As children, we craved structure. Like any children, we wanted to butt up against immovable rules and systems that would help us self-regulate. But those didn't exist. Instead, it was a years-long free-for-all of mayhem, punctuated by our mom self-harming, and our dad telling us we were worthless. There was a carousel of chore assignments and attempts at structure that disintegrated mere hours after they were conceived. We were not taught to take a shower, or speak kindly. They created artificial divisions: older against younger, boys against girls, and worthy against unworthy. Instead of regarding each other as siblings, or family, we were these labels.

In my perception as a child, the dysfunction was set up so that there were the boys, the girls, and then me. There were the parents, the children, and then me. Of course, in truth, every single child was isolated, othered, and made to feel separate and less worthy. But this happens to be where I am sharing my own experience – one of profound otherness.

Once there was an overabundance of children, one bedroom was assigned for the boys, one bedroom was for the girls, and I was relegated to a mattress in the living room, sleeping next to the dog. I belonged with no one, and was scapegoated for most of the family's problems.

This culminated into a sense of not being a person. I wasn't allowed to be. I was blamed for the family's problems, but also demonized for trying to fix them. I had to be a hero – I had to be perfect, anticipate everyone's needs, and guard against all bad outcomes. And the moment I failed to be perfect, I was a villain instead. Blamed for the behaviors of my siblings, blamed for the financial struggles of my parents, and blamed for pointing out things that should change.

In the face of the deep denial that blinded her to the abuse in the home, my mother had some odd ways of offering comfort. Once, she took me aside and told me about a vision she had. "When I was pregnant with you, I was scared, and I didn't know what to do," she said. "But then one day, I was praying, and I suddenly got a vision of you. In the vision you were happy, and healthy. You were okay." She shared the story of this prophetic vision as if it absolved her of any need to protect me.

"How old was I, in the vision?" I asked.

"You were fully grown up. Like an adult," she replied.

An adult. I took this to heart. Many times in my childhood, when I faced fear or uncertainty, I would remember this story – this myth of immortality – and think, *Well, at least I know I don't die here. The vision showed that I live to at least 18.*

I was constantly on the lookout for disaster, always guarding against any crisis I could imagine. I'd yank my siblings back from ledges and balconies, check everyone's seatbelts, and make sure I didn't lose anyone when we were out in public. Once, when I was 13, we were listening to the news anxiously as a tornado terrorized the next town over. The reporters were suddenly astonished – the tornado had vanished. We listened intently, waiting to hear where it would touch down again. Then the sky outside of our window went black. We rushed to the bathroom to huddle and wait out the storm. Then, we realized something – we didn't have the youngest kid. I and two of my brothers sprinted to our parents' room where the one-year-old was napping on the bed. The wind was screaming outside. I grabbed her, and we made it back to the bathroom. Then the whole house shook. The massive oak tree in the front yard was torn from its roots, and crashed through the roof, slamming down on the bed our sister was on moments prior.

Five years later, we were at a carnival, and we boarded a ride called the 'Twister'. Apparently fate wanted to test us again. The ride was one of those elevated spinners – you sat in a seat attached to a pod attached to the hub. Three seats to a pod, three pods to the hub, and each rotated around the others while tilting high above the carnival. I sat next to my sisters, and as we reached the apex of the ride, dangling over the machinery, my youngest sister's seatbelt silently slipped off and twirled to the ground. I reached over from my seat and grabbed her tightly by the shirt. She slipped downward as the ride spun, and the only thing keeping her from being tossed to the ground was my grip. My knuckles were white as I prayed she didn't slip out of her clothes, and the next three minutes felt like an eternity.

The ride came to a stop. We told our parents what happened. Our dad shrugged. Our mom gasped in that familiar way that meant *This is too stressful to hear about* instead of *I'm glad you're okay.*

We would often joke that a third 'twister' will eventually arrive and claim our youngest sister.

Vacations were rare for the family, and even rarer for me. Once, when I was 10 years old, we took a week-long trip to Destin, Florida to stay in a condo graciously opened to us by a considerate family from church. The first day, I discovered the ocean, and fell in love. An isolated child, I had never really spent time at the beach before, and I was not a strong swimmer. Even still, I would take the boogie board, paddle out as far as I could go, and blissfully crash back to shore with the biggest wave I could find. I did that over and over, for hours and hours. No one checked on me, no one counseled me on water safety, and no one wondered where I was.

The tide changed midday, and suddenly I found myself no longer crashing back to shore. I was being pulled farther out into the ocean. Clutching my little boogie board, I realized I could no longer see the beach at all. I was afraid, but I remembered the 'prophecy' from my mother. I knew that I would live to at least 18. I held on, and waited.

A passing boater happened to see me.

"Hey, uh, you need some help?"

I was a child, floating in the middle of the ocean. "Yeah."

I held on to the side of the boat as he towed me to shore. I landed on the beach, gasping, and a little disoriented. I didn't know how the ocean had suddenly betrayed me.

Walking up the beach, I found my family. They were having lunch, and didn't take much notice of my return.

Minutes later, I was back in the ocean. More careful this time, I only went out as far as it seemed I could paddle myself back. I did that for hours more, until the sun was setting.

Exhausted, I went back up the shoreline and found the steps to the beach house we were staying at. And then the pain set in. No one had put sunscreen on me, and I, as sheltered as I was at 10 years old, did not even know it was important. I broke out into second degree burns all over my body. I was purple from burns, and in immense agony. While everyone else was enjoying time in the water, I spent the next week at the beach blistering, alternating between the bed and the bath, soaking in aloe. In retrospect, I probably should have seen a doctor.

My other siblings would occasionally go on trips with a friend who invited them to travel with their family, or their godparents who treated them to a fun extended weekend. I didn't have those. I did have some camping trips with my uncle and cousins, and I treasured those outings.

One Summer, my family was all packed up and getting ready to leave for a trip to Virginia, to spend a week at the lake with our cousins. I was 14 years old, and had put some clothes in a bag and began the inevitable negotiation with my siblings of who would claim what seat for the trip. I much preferred the back seat, far from my parents, where I could stretch out and read my books.

My parents caught me packing. "Oh, you're not coming," my mother blankly informed me.

"There's not enough room in the van for all you fuckin' kids," my dad complained.

They explained that even though there were enough seats in the family van for everyone normally, there weren't enough with all of the luggage. And as the oldest, I was the only one who could fend for myself at home. They loaded up the van and left. I spent the next week at home, alone.

I think it was that same year that we were awarded "Family of the Year" from our church. Our parents would put on a brilliant show at church, speaking to us softly and beaming with pride at their gaggle of children. They volunteered whenever possible, teaching liturgy or cooking community dinners. Everyone admired us. The plaque, celebrating us for being an example of love and virtue, hung on the wall between the paddle our dad would beat us with and a hole the shape of my body.

6

BUT ONCE A YEAR

Christmas day was a precious time for everyone. For other children, the magic of Christmas was in the decor, the food, and the presents. For us, the magic of Christmas was that it was the one day a year with no violence. Our dad would be kinder that day, and exude a patience that was missing from every other day. We were gentle with each other, too. Christmas was truly a day of magic, and we treasured it.

On every other day of the year, I escaped into books and games.

I begged to go to the library as often as I could – the same local library I had been visiting since I learned to read. Blackshear Place Library was a haven for me – I would get stacks of books every week, and tear through them at lightning speed. *The Chronicles of Narnia, The Chronicles of Prydain, The Wizard of Oz, The Phantom Tollbooth* – anything that took the characters to another world took me there too. I'd also check out computer games, books on tape, comic books – anything I could find.

My first introduction to video games was from the Gorslines when I was three. They had an original Nintendo Entertainment System, and I would watch in awe as they showed off every secret and shortcut in *Super Mario Bros*. We never had that system at home, but my grandparents got one to have at their house for the grandkids to play when we would get together on the holidays.

The Super Nintendo was the latest video game system in the early 90s, but we didn't get one. Then, just in time for Christmas 1996, the Nintendo 64 was released. The 3D graphics looked magical, and every advertisement in stores showcased the return of Mario. But Christmas Day came, and there was no Nintendo 64.

Over the course of that next year, I reveled in the stories from the kids at church about their games. *Super Mario 64, Mario Kart, Star Wars*. It seemed like a portal to a new world, like the kinds I had read about in books.

Each Christmas was more extravagant than the last in our house – seeming proof that Santa Claus had to be real, as our parents could have never afforded everything that appeared Christmas morning. Santa Claus was our savior, bringing peace to Earth, and we worshiped him. In truth, our parents were going into more debt, and the luxury and peace of that day stood in stark contrast to every other day of the year.

And then Christmas 1997 came. Deluxe play kitchen sets, new bikes, and name-brand clothes flowed from under the tree. I had gotten some socks and a couple books. Once all the gifts had been opened ravenously, we started cleaning up the wrapping paper. My mom gestured to a box hidden away in the back of the tree. I immediately suspected what it was, and excitedly opened it. A Nintendo 64.

Every day that I played the Nintendo 64 was like Christmas again. Even today, mere images of the game cartridges and controllers evoke a powerful nostalgia that nothing else comes close to.

It wasn't just digital games, though. My granddad maintained a collection of board games in his garage that I would gravitate towards every time I visited. *Othello, Bolt 'n' Stein, Enchanted Forest, Master Labyrinth, Mastermind*. They were enigmas – puzzles to solve and master.

I loved mastering systems and rulesets – an antidote to the chaos of the house. I would study guidebooks of origami and string figures. I followed detailed tutorials on constructing castles out of cardboard. Each Christmas would grow my collection of logic deduction puzzles, riddles, mazes, and magic tricks, and I would time myself to master them as quickly as possible.

And then, when I was eight years old, came the logic puzzle that I would regret for a very long time.

I had a sneaking awareness that something about Christmas didn't fully add up. *Santa is of course real,* I thought to myself. *But it doesn't hurt to verify it.* So I turned to my mom.

"Is Santa real?" I asked her.

She paused for a moment, deciding what to say. "What do you think? Do you think he's real?" she finally responded.

In that moment, I regretted asking the question. *I should have been more specific. I should have asked how Santa flies, or how he visits so many houses in one night, or whether the elves are compensated fairly.*

Even still, the logic puzzle was already unfolding in my head. *If Santa is real, and I say yes, she'll confirm it. If Santa is real and I say no, she'll correct me and tell me he is in fact real. But if Santa is not real and I say yes, she would most likely maintain the illusion she's maintained so far, and tell me I'm right. Even though I still believe Santa is real, the only way to gain new knowledge in this scenario is to tell her that I don't believe in Santa, so she will either tell me I'm wrong or confess the truth.*

"No, I don't think he's real," I lied.

"That's right," she said, with a slight smile.

I was devastated.

7

INTO THE WOODS

My mother restricted me from consuming media that she deemed dangerous or corrupting – at least, until she got reassurance from the other moms at church that something was permissible. We did not have cable TV, and could only watch educational shows on PBS. I could not watch movies rated PG until I was 13, and I couldn't watch movies rated PG-13 until I was 17.

The rare exceptions were the Lord of the Rings films. I had read all the books by the time I was 10, spurred on by my granddad who had read them in his youth. The first film was released when I was 11. After much pleading and negotiation, I was allowed to see it in theaters with a boy from church and his mom. It was my first time seeing a film in theaters, and it was transformative. It was a story of purpose, and of great perseverance to thwart evil. It was about the power of community in the face of despair, and surviving under the oppressive gaze of a hateful eye.

That same year, we started attending Prince of Peace Catholic Church, and I saw that they were casting for a children's play: *The Hobbit*. I had of course read *The Hobbit* and loved it, and the idea of being *in* one of my favorite stories was irresistible, so I asked if I could audition.

I arrived at the meeting with the director. It turned out that I was auditioning late – as I walked in, the rest of the cast were leaving the first rehearsal. Even still, it seemed they needed more actors, so she had me read some lines for her. She told me I would be cast as Thorin Oakenshield, King under the Mountain. They had run out of scripts, but I took one home anyway – another young actor had left it behind after the rehearsal, and would be given a different one later. It was in a green folder, with that child's name scribbled in the corner.

As the weeks went on, one of the nice parents helped me practice my lines. I struggled to memorize everything as easily as I thought I should, but the show went on and I did just fine. One of my sisters was in it as well. It was lovely to be part of something, and even lovelier to share something with a sibling without the weight of hostility and suspicion that permeated everything we shared at home.

My dad sneered at the idea of me being involved in theater. It wasn't masculine enough, and it was made very clear that he would only respect someone being involved with contact sports or hard labor. My brothers were playing football and going with him on construction jobs, but I had no interest in anything that seemed like it would make me more like him. My compromise was joining Boy Scouts.

The local scout troop was obsessed with camping. There were no initiatives to use the merit badge handbooks, or get involved in community service. There was simply a camping trip every other weekend, year-round – and camping in February is not fun at all. I think the scoutmaster and his buddies wanted an excuse to leave their wives for a weekend. Any excuse to leave the house was fine with me too, and I quickly adapted to the primitive excursions.

I learned how to handle knives, shoot arrows, build shelters, and most excitingly, make fire. Making fire is quite grounding for me, even to this day. I would methodically collect all the needed types of wood: tinder, kindling, and fuelwood. I would carefully arrange them into a tepee shape, and stoke the fire for hours, moving logs and optimizing the amount of oxygen available to the embers. Another puzzle to master.

Once, while on a camping trip, it was perfectly temperate weather and we all decided to sleep in hammocks instead of in tents. I left my boots below my hammock, and dozed under the stars. The next morning, I slipped my boots on without looking. Pain seized my toes. I yelped and ripped them off quickly, and a family of scorpions tumbled out. Even to this day, I now habitually check the insides of my shoes every single time I put them on.

One summer, when I was 14 years old, our troop attended a Boy Scout summer camp event: two weeks in the woods with nearly a hundred other troops, all competing in events and attending merit badge classes. My parents were more than happy to have one less kid at home for two weeks.

The first week of camp, it rained intensely for days on end. Our tents were swamps, and there was no way to get dry. We were shivering, soggy, and had almost no food because we could not cook over a fire in the rain. On day five of the rain, I asked to go to the camp headquarters and call my parents. My dad answered the phone.

"Please come and get me. It's raining and miserable here. I want to come home," I pleaded.

"No, you're fine there, don't be a fuckin' baby. I gotta go."

He hung up.

The next week of camp had more sun. I attended a knot-tying class and a first aid class. Then, there was an open call to sign up for a new challenge: head a mile into the woods with only a compass and a flashlight, survive for 36 hours, and then hike back. The idea of doing that certainly sounded miserable, but I wanted to prove that I was capable of accomplishing difficult things – that I hadn't pleaded to go home because I couldn't handle suffering. I wasn't a baby. Besides, that vision from my mother rang in my head. *At least I know it won't kill me. I definitely live until I'm at least an adult*, I told myself.

Two other scouts and I volunteered for the mission, and our parents were called to give consent. We hiked into the woods, alone. Together, we built a rudimentary shelter from downed trees and branches, and we built a fire. We cooperated well together. The next day, we just sat in the woods, and chatted. We had no food, and weren't skilled enough to do any hunting. We starved for a day, but I was used to being hungry. We slept again in our shelter. First thing in the morning, we hiked back to camp.

People seemed surprised to see us. We had our photo taken, and an article was written about us in the local paper. I was happy to get breakfast.

When not camping with the scouts, I still found that I slept better outside. I would make a tent out of a tarp in the backyard, and spend nights out there alone, with just a flashlight and a book. I often made homemade bows and arrows from the woods around our house. I would forage for hours, finding a perfectly flexible piece of wood. I'd trim off the twigs, and carve notches into the ends. Then I would use string to pull the wood back into a recurve shape, and whittle arrows from thin sticks. They would fly surprisingly accurately, and I challenged myself with targets at increasing distances. I made dozens of these, refining the craft. It made me feel capable, like I could survive on my own if I needed to. I was always bracing for the moment my family would abandon me, and work like this made me feel prepared.

I found many ways to occupy myself in my childhood when I wasn't reading books, playing games, or camping, and some were more stupid than others. My granddad was an electrical engineer, and he had a workshop in his garage filled with wires and circuits and motors. When I was 12, I had intuited the basics of electrical current from watching him, and wanted to experiment on my own. When he was distracted, I snuck into his workshop and started working. I got an old extension cord he had thrown away, and cut it in half. This revealed two thick wires inside, coiled around each other. I straightened them, frayed the ends, and attached each to metal clips. This resulted in a cord with a plug on one end, and two clips on the other. Then I got aluminum foil from the kitchen, and packed it tightly into a solid sphere, larger than my fist. I smuggled my nefarious creations home in my backpack.

When I got home, I excitedly raced into the bathroom and shut the door. I pulled at two ends of the foil ball, and made two poles for the clips to connect to. I connected the clips to the two poles, completing the circuit. There I stood, a solid ball of aluminum in one hand, and the plug in the other. I wanted to know what would happen. Would the ball glow?

There are three incredibly stupid gambles I've taken in my life that should have ended in total disaster, but somehow didn't – this was the first, and stupidest. In a move far more foolish than any 12 year old has any right in making, I plugged the cord into the bathroom outlet.

There was a brief, blinding flash of blue arcing plasma, and then darkness. The electrical breaker had been tripped. In a house as old and poorly maintained as ours, the fact that the breaker worked correctly is a miracle. If it hadn't, I likely would not be here to write this story today. Experiment complete, I examined myself. No harm, except for a strange tingling feeling. I surreptitiously disposed of my metal and wire abomination with a strange mix of shame and pride. I had succeeded, in a way. I had created something powerful with tools, like my grandfather knew how to do. And I had proven my immortality once again.

The land we lived on was surrounded by farmland, and our property was likely farmland itself at one point. The backyard would seem small to an adult, but to me as a child it was massive. It had rolling hills and groves of trees, honeysuckle bushes, and endless places to hide and corners to explore.

One day, during my eleventh summer, I was surveying a dig that my brothers were conducting in the backyard. I spied a glint of metal poking up from the dirt. I took a shovel and dug more, and finally the strange object released from the ground. It was a twisted piece of black metal, about as long as my arm. I was fascinated by this. *Was our backyard once the site of an ancient ritual? Is this treasure once buried by pirates?* The object had clearly been broken. I kept digging, and found another piece. I laid them side by side. It almost looked like a puzzle.

Every day that summer I returned to the yard, digging as much as I could. Over time I amassed an impressive collection of these metal artifacts. I kept them assembled like a jigsaw puzzle, laid out flat on the ground. The metal curved in odd, nearly symmetrical ways, and many pieces fit snugly together. My mind would spin with the possibilities. *Perhaps if I find every piece, something magical will happen. Or maybe it will reveal a riddle, etched into the metal, waiting to be solved.* Looking back on it, it's clear that this was merely some sort of garden gate or metal decor that had been disposed of improperly. But to me, it was the ultimate quest.

After two months, I had nearly finished it. I had dug everywhere, finding new pieces of this strange object scattered across the yard. And then one day, I went out, determined to find the final piece – and it was gone. My dad had thrown it all away.

"Why?" I asked.

The reply came with a raised hand. "You need to spend less time dicking around in the yard and more time doing something actually fuckin' useful for once."

One late spring afternoon, I was coming home from school, prodding a tender welt under my eye. My dad had thrown me into a bedframe the day before, and it had left a mark. This wasn't typical – he was usually very careful to never leave visible bruises that might make anyone at school suspicious, and would boast about that skill regularly.

As I walked up the driveway, something was waiting for me. A rusty dirt bike – an off-road motorcycle sized for kids – was parked in the gravel.

My dad handed me the key. "Here. Buddy of mine found this in a fuckin' trash heap and fixed it up. You can give it a go."

I reached for the key tentatively. He snatched it back, saying, "But it's mine, not yours, you hear me? Don't go fuckin' it up."

This was an apology, in a way, for leaving a visible welt. It was the only thing I could remember him ever giving me. Just another example of his dramatic mood shifts, and I wondered what karmic pain this meant was waiting for me tomorrow. Still, I hoped to not disappoint him.

I straddled the bike, engine sputtering. The throttle was in my right hand. I held my breath, and pulled. The bike ripped forward, and I zipped across the yard faster than I had expected. The bike quickly slid to the left, and went spinning as I spilled off to the right. I cried out, grasping at a fresh gash of blood on my leg. My dad snorted and rolled his eyes, stomping off to have another beer.

I avoided the bike for several days. But eventually, it started to feel like yet another puzzle to solve. A wild dog to tame. So one day, I slid open the splintered wellhouse door and wheeled out the bike. I started it up, and balanced on top. I pulled the throttle slowly this time, feeling the bike lurch forward. Nearly every day for three months I rode that bike, obsessing over mastering it. Soon enough I was tearing through the yard and into the woods, banking on tight turns, nearly hugging my body to the ground as I raced around groves of trees. It became about control. Every single shift of weight to one side, every ounce of power to the engine, every calculated risk of momentum over rocks and roots – a system entirely in my control. This was power. This was where no one could touch me, no one could catch me, and if I got hurt it was no one else's gambit but mine.

I came home from school, and the bike was gone. The door to the wellhouse hung askew, and the front door was busted in. Someone had invaded our house, taking the TV and the dirt bike. There wasn't much else to take. I was crestfallen.

"Shit fuckin' happens," my dad said. "I bet you fuckin' left it out where they could see it, didn't you?"

Another summer, we attended a festival as a family. There was live music, and plenty of space for running around. Vendors were selling crafts and homemade goods. In one corner of the fairgrounds, though, someone was giving away newborn rabbits. I begged to take a rabbit home. "No" came the immediate reply from both parents.

I should have known better by this point – of course they wouldn't say yes if I asked. I pulled one of my brothers aside, and told him how special it would be if we had a pet rabbit at home. His eyes grew wide, and he ran to ask our parents if we could take one home. "Yes" came the reply.

We picked out a pure black rabbit, and I named him Shadow. Shadow lived in a large cage in our backyard. Every day for months I would go outside with carrots and lettuce, and play with Shadow. I loved that rabbit, and we became very good friends.

Then one day, I went out with a pocketful of carrots, and the cage was empty. I was horrified. I was worried he would be eaten by something much larger.

I ran back inside to let everyone know about the emergency. "Shadow escaped!" I said, hoping to inspire everyone to mount a rescue mission. My dad sat there with a beer in his hand, rolling his eyes.

"I sent him into the woods," he said. " You don't need a fuckin' rabbit, you need to fuckin' clean up your shit around here."

8

DOWN THE HATCH

Ever since I was young, I have had problems with my esophagus. Food gets uncomfortably stuck on the way down, somewhere between being swallowed and actually landing in my stomach. I had countless appointments with gastrointestinal doctors and specialists, and multiple endoscopies to probe for the exact issue. I spent two weeks at Scottish Rite Hospital in Atlanta under observation, as they did countless tests on my digestive system.

They offered several theories. I was told that I lacked motility: the peristalsis of the esophagus that is meant to push food down either didn't work or spasmed randomly. I was told I had achalasia: the opening from the esophagus to the stomach was narrowed and refused to let food pass. I was told I had reflux: the acid washing up into my esophagus caused inflammation and swelling, limiting its ability to carry food.

Not given much sensible information, I developed many of my own theories. One theory I had is that it could be an autonomic issue – a failure of the automatic nervous system to send the right signals. I have several issues with my autonomic system. I wet the bed until I was 11. I often stop breathing at night. I even stop breathing during the day if I am overly focused or stressed, and end up choking and gasping for air. When I am anxious, my bowels shut down and refuse to let anything happen down there until I calm down. I wondered if the uselessness of my esophagus is a failure of my autonomic system, stemming from childhood trauma.

Either way, ultimately I was told around age 13 that my body was simply broken, and the only solution was a surgical procedure to inflate my esophagus with a balloon. This would allow anything to pass through, but also permit acid to travel up to my throat at a high rate. I opted out of this, as the idea of a surgery with permanent downsides scared me.

Instead, I've just lived with it for my entire life so far. I chew my food carefully. I chase every bite with water to force the food down, and feel as it squeezes through the narrow opening and pops into my stomach. Sometimes, food has a particular density or texture that doesn't cooperate well. Things like white meat and bread will expand when doused with the following swallow of water, rather than break apart. This can result in a swollen bolus of food lodged in place. Because of this I've had to get several emergency endoscopies as a teen and an adult, to have food removed from my esophagus. My last one as of this writing was in 2014, when I was 23. To complicate matters, I had an extremely negative reaction to the Propofol used to sedate me. I had delayed emergence from the anesthesia, and was nearly comatose for a week after the procedure. I could be roused to drink liquids or go to the bathroom, but my vision was blurred, my memory was flickering, I was confused, and I went straight back to bed afterwards. It was described as a Propofol 'allergy' but could be a neurological issue. I was instructed to never take Propofol again.

To avoid the hospital visit and the anesthesia involved in removing stuck food with surgery, I have developed some rather bizarre techniques for doing it myself. First, I swallow water, and bear down to hold it in as long as I can on top of that stuck food. It eventually regurgitates painfully, but it does so with small shreds of food. I would do this over and over, peeling off bits of the food to break it up gradually. Then, I'll walk my feet up a wall and stand upside down with my hands on the ground. I will force myself to retch and attempt to use gravity to get something out. It's disgusting and painful, but has avoided multiple close calls of needing surgical removal of food.

It wouldn't be until I was 33 that I discovered more. After a particular nasty episode, I requested my full medical records from when I was a child. In those records, I discovered a theory about my swallowing disorder that they never told me: it could be food allergies. The records showed a diagnosis of eosinophilia, which at the time was merely described to me as "swelling resulting from acid reflux."

Now, decades later, I've done some research and learned that eosinophilia can also arise from food allergies – crucial information that was never told to me when I was a child. Another truth about my world that the adults around me didn't take pains to investigate.

Having never had any kind of difficulty breathing after eating, I had always assumed that I have no food allergies. I got tested, though, and I am apparently severely allergic to wheat – with minor allergies to milk, soy, corn, and oats. I have eaten all those foods daily for years, not knowing I was allergic to them, and simply tolerating the array of digestive and skin issues that accompanied it. Constant constipation, difficulty swallowing, and even the bed-wetting in my youth are all explained by allergies.

Still, as a child, I wondered about my biological father. Did he have this issue too? Was there some quirk of genetics that could reveal blessed truths about how my own body worked? Somewhere out there, I imagined, was the man who fled from me as a baby, holding those secrets.

9

POTATO PANCAKES

I only met the family on my dad's side twice. We took two trips up to Ohio to visit them, and it was miserable both times. No one was warm, or inquisitive. The adults argued whenever possible, and the children would fight and break things. My dad's parents died of some combination of alcohol abuse and drug overdose when he was young, and he and his siblings had been taken in by a family member and raised alongside his cousins and half-cousins. Many people in his family were consumed by addiction, and violence and petty crime were their way of life.

I grew up knowing cousins on my mom's side pretty well. Every year I'd excitedly look forward to Thanksgiving and Fourth of July, when I'd get to see our extended family. They came from Virginia and South Carolina to stay for a week at a time with our grandparents. In the summer, I would go with my granddad to pick blackberries on the side of a nearby road, and we'd haul them back in buckets to make pies. Thanksgiving was always warm and safe – Granddad would carefully tend to the turkey in the oven, and there was a flurry of activity as everyone made the rest of the food.

My mom's two brothers, my uncles, were idols for me. I was always asking my Uncle Jim what his favorite movie or book was that year, so I could make it my favorite too. He had an infectious laugh, and I felt a kinship with him as an oldest sibling. My Uncle Steve took a special interest in me, and impacted my childhood more than he probably knew. Steve would take me to yard sales to scavenge for bargain bin computer parts, and I'd help him assemble it like an electronic frankenstein. He'd then send me home with the computer, and the next year we'd do it again, searching yard sales for upgrades and new parts.

It was thanks to Steve that not only did I have a computer, but I knew how it was built. I would break the computer at least once a year by treating it like a puzzle and experimenting with the system's settings, and he'd kindly fix it up and give it back. From there I learned web design and programming – skills I never would have built without him.

Steve's Thanksgiving ritual was to hunt through the newspaper for the best Black Friday deals: he'd giggle gleefully when spotting anything that had "free after rebate" in small print. He'd make a list, sketch out a plan of attack, and give me my mission. The next morning, we'd wake up at four in the morning – Steve, his son Andrew, and me. We'd wait in line outside at Fry's Electronics, waiting for the doors to open. Then we'd rush in, and exact our plan. Within minutes we'd each have a full cart. Steve would complete the purchase, and on the way home with my loot in my lap, we'd all tell our glory stories of how we pulled it off as if it was a heist.

Perhaps, though, what I most admired about Jim and Steve was that they were *hilarious*. Jokes and puns flowed constantly. Their sense of humor was influenced in turn by Granddad, who was very funny in his own right, and always had a quip ready to go. In many ways, the dinner table at holidays was an improv game, with suggestions and set ups flying across the table, waiting for someone else to nail the punchline and get the whole table laughing.

My aunt Eileen had six kids, and in many ways my six siblings and I perceived them as foils to us. Visiting with them was like looking out of a funhouse mirror into the real world – a world where parents provided structure and encouragement.

The oldests of all three families – Andrew, me, and Eileen's Daniel – had a special bond. Our grandmother called us her three musketeers – a designation we wore with pride.

My grandmother and grandfather were special to me. Mamaw and Granddad, I called them. Mamaw is the only person who ever even remotely taught me manners.

"Chew with your mouth closed," she'd say. "It's yes, not yup." "Look both ways before crossing the street." Some of these concepts seemed old-fashioned to me as a kid, but her suggestions were never stifling or sneering. Moreover, having someone take an interest in me and provide any kind of guidance was welcome.

Mamaw would write stories about 'monkeydogs' that lived on the ceiling, and other whimsical creatures – her clever inventions to get a squirming child to look up when washing their hair, for example.

She also encouraged me to write. She signed me up for a youth poetry contest, where the winners would get published in an anthology of children's poetry. I treated it like a puzzle to be solved, and I was determined to win – not with authentic expression, but by appealing to the judges. I wrote three poems. One, a humorous poem about how my esophagus doesn't work correctly. One, a surreal romp through a fantasy land. And the last one, a sappy patriotic poem titled "Land, Air, and Sea". I rolled my eyes as I penned the final words, injecting every pandering sentiment I could feign for America. All three were winners, and were published in the book.

I spent as much time with Mamaw as I could. She started getting sick, and was increasingly bed-bound for long stretches of time. I sat with her every weekend, reading stories and chatting.

Granddad was my hero. I would escape to his house any night I could. We'd stay up late watching Scooby-Doo and eating ice cream. The next morning, he'd make me his signature potato pancakes. These potato pancakes were the ultimate prize of visiting Granddad's house – on holidays, we'd all excitedly beg to be at his house for breakfast. In truth, it was merely potato flakes mixed into pancake batter, but it was our ambrosia. It was our bread from heaven.

Granddad was someone who took care of me without complaint. He considered what I may need, and provided it without raging about how 'undeserving' I was. That was a paternal energy I did not have at home.

Looking back, I can see a more full picture of the man he was. He was attentive, and caretaking. But, he never once said "I love you" to me. He never hugged me. I don't think that way of caring for someone was accessible to him. I can see now how that was the same father my mom and her siblings had. And I can see how that left a mark on their childhood – especially my mom's. But for me, the ability to eat breakfast without being scared I was going to be hit, and the experience of merely watching TV and laughing together – that was the safety I craved, and I didn't know anything else was missing.

One day, as a preteen, things had gotten pretty bad at home. My dad had thrown me around for a bit, knocking me through another wall.

"If you don't like it, you can fuckin' leave!" he hollered through the hole in the plaster.

So, I called his bluff. With tears in my eyes, I stuffed some clothes in a bag and set off down the road. I didn't have a plan of where I was going, but I was resolved to make it on the streets or in the woods on my own. I could survive with very little, I had proven that. Besides, I knew I would survive – the vision from my mother assured it. My mom, panicking, didn't know what to do; so, she called my granddad.

I got a half mile from the house, when he appeared in his car.

"Get in the car, Alex." he said.

My cousin Andrew was in the backseat. I was startled by this. I hadn't known he was in town. *Could this be my rescue?* I wondered. I imagined him as an emissary from the extended family, witnessing the truth and the pain. I imagined them staging a triumphant intervention, shielding my siblings and me from any further violence.

"I am never going back there!" I seethed.

"Get in the car!" my granddad said, forcefully.

I got in the car, sobbing.

He drove me home, and got out to speak to my dad. Andrew sat in the car, a young boy horrified by the drama unfolding. There was a lot of yelling. My granddad still did not know the extent of the abuse, but even still I had never heard someone speak up for me like that. He scolded my dad for being harsh, and for driving me away. I held my breath, watching this collision of worlds, waiting for either my dad's wrath to explode in a crescendo of new violence, or for him to be humbled by the lecture. Neither happened. He just made some nasty remarks, and left sulking to have a beer.

Things didn't change too much after that. The magical rescue from the family never came, and my parents just got better at hiding the abuse. But for at least a couple days, my dad avoided me.

It was soon after that, when I was 13, my family decided to adopt a Golden Retriever. My dad made a plan to go and get the puppy, but needed someone to ride with him to hold onto the dog on the way home. I was elected to do so, and neither my dad nor I were happy about this. We didn't speak on the way there.

The puppy mill was disgusting and flea-ridden. Still, we got the puppy that was set aside for us. The puppy's mother was named Queen, so I named him Prince. He rode in my lap the whole way home, scratching.

The difference between my dad and my granddad was stark, and played out in many situations over my childhood.

When I turned 16, my Uncle Steve gave me my first car. It was a beater – a 1988 GMC Jimmy that leaked oil constantly and vibrated so loud you could hardly have a conversation inside. Even still, I was immensely grateful. My granddad taught me to drive, and got me my license. He did so without being asked, and without complaint. Meanwhile, my dad reminded me that the car was not mine – it belonged to him because I was a minor, and he would take it away anytime he wanted. My granddad encouraged me to get my first job, and I did: Member Services at Lake Lanier Islands Resort. I worked there two summers in a row, printing season passes, and handling customer complaints at the waterpark. My dad levied a tax on my wages, claiming it was restitution for being a bad son.

One day, my youngest brother was angry. He had every right to be, as he was channeling the anger from our dad, and given no outlet for it. He was outside, picking an argument with his older sister. He started to scream in a rage, and picked up a golf club. Swinging it over his head, he threw it as hard as it could. It crashed through the back windshield of my GMC Jimmy, shattering the glass. My dad screamed at me for not stopping my brother. My granddad helped me seal the back window with film and tape.

My dad continually took money from my granddad. He would claim it was needed to finally add a new bedroom to the house and make more room for the kids. Seasons came and went, and there was no sign of any work on the house. Then he'd blame it on surprise bills, and borrow more money from Granddad. In truth, he was drinking the money away, wasting it on alcohol.

When I was a teenager, Granddad often had me come over after school and mow his lawn, weed the garden, and other landscaping projects. He'd pay me 10 dollars an hour – money that more often than not was seized by my dad as 'payment' for the privilege of living in his house, or reparations for some invented bad behavior. Towards the end of one summer, I was 15 years old and feeling especially bitter about never having enough money. Feeling blamed for the money problems in the family.

And then came the third and final time I stole something. One day after coming in from mowing his lawn, I spied Granddad's wallet sitting on his dresser. I opened it. Two wrinkled 20 dollar bills were inside. I took them, feeling the pangs of shame as soon as I did it. When I got home, the realization struck me – I was no different from my dad. I stole granddad's money, just like he did. I was too ashamed to bring it back to him and face him for what I did, but I never stole anything again.

10

IN MY DEFENSE

During my seventh grade year, my mother was pregnant with her seventh child. I was ostensibly being homeschooled, but I did no schoolwork that year, and there was not even an attempt to provide me with a curriculum. Instead, I just read books.

My mother had her seventh child, and her reproductive system seemed to rebel in the process. She had to have an emergency hysterectomy right after the baby was born. If she didn't, there's no telling how many children she would have continued to have.

With seven kids in the house and money at an all time low, the fundamentalist principles my parents held on to buckled and gave out. My mom sent us all back to public school, and she went back to work as a speech therapist in the school system. I entered the eighth grade with the reading ability of a college student, and the social ability of a fourth grader. I was incredibly socially stunted, but still tried to make friends. I was awkward, with confidence only being summoned when I would answer questions in class.

One day early in the year, my mother arrived to pick me up early from school. Her brother Jim was with her.

"We need to go see Mamaw," she said. "She doesn't have much time left."

I had known this was coming. She had been sick for a long time. We arrived at the house, and went inside. Granddad was there, by her bedside. As I walked in the room, she took her last breath.

At the funeral, Andrew and Daniel and I delivered a poem that I wrote titled "The Three Musketeers," detailing her nickname for us, and our love for her. I cried through the whole thing. I had lost one of the few people who showed me genuine care.

Back at school and reeling from the loss, I found it much easier to relate to girls than to boys. I wasn't conscious of it at the time, but male figures scared me – even peers. I observed my peers like a Martian visiting Earth. I studied their social performances, seeing clearly the patterns and invisible rules, but not having any way to participate.

There was a trio of girls in most of my classes who were extremely bookish and goofy, always singing songs in the hallway and scribbling notes to pass during class. One was quite funny, one overtly sarcastic, and one very quiet. I attached myself to them, and quickly developed a crush on the quiet one.

We had to choose an elective class – either Chorus, Art, or Band. I chose Chorus merely because that was where the Singing Trio was. I was not a good singer. There was an after-school drama club advertised, and sure enough, the Singing Trio signed up gleefully. I remembered the play of *The Hobbit* from church fondly, and followed suit. I was cast as a lead role in *The Orphan Train*. They needed a young girl to join for a special role, and once again I encouraged my sister to audition – the same sister that acted in *The Hobbit* with me. She landed the part, and we shared the stage once again. Another precious moment of feeling connected to a sibling.

I hovered around that group of girls as often as I could, until one day, the quiet one passed me a note.

"Do you want to be my boyfriend?" the note read.

I was elated. *"Yes"* I scribbled back.

I was overcome with the idea that someone valued me; that someone was giving me a chance to prove myself. I needed to show her how much I could love her. I needed to be worth her time, but not waste it. Every night, I would go home and write her pages and pages of poetry about how much I loved her and how beautiful she was. Then each morning, I would give her what I'd written, and then sheepishly avoid her the rest of the day. I wouldn't look at her, or hold her hand, or speak more than a couple words to her.

The antisocial love-bombing lasted about a week. One of the other girls came up to me at the end of the week, and said, "She is breaking up with you."

I did not understand what I could have possibly done wrong, at the time. I had expressed the deepest love possible, and still it felt like it was not enough. I went home and cried.

For that entire year of eighth grade, I was tormented by bullies. The most aggressive one was on the bus. He lived on my road, in a house somehow smaller than mine. He had been held back a grade and I had skipped a grade, so he was a full year older than me and several inches taller than me. I should have pitied him, but instead I was terrified of him. It didn't matter where I sat on the bus, every day he would sit behind me. He would loudly berate me for being ugly, or worthless. He would make fun of my large ears, and call me satellite boy. I tolerated this in silence every day, staring at the seat in front of me. Near the end of the school year, he escalated things. Apparently tired of me ignoring him, he started threatening me.

"I'll punch you in the head, and you won't do anything. Will you? Will you? You won't do anything."

I still sat there, staring ahead, giving him no reaction.

He finally grew too tired of getting no reaction, and he reached forward over the bus seat, and punched me in the ear as hard as he could.

My ears were ringing, and adrenaline flooded my body.

I have only physically enacted violence on someone three times in my life – and this would be the first.

I stood up, stepped into the aisle, and turned to face him. He chuckled at that.

"What are you gonna–" he couldn't finish the sentence.

I balled my fists, locked my elbows, and slammed my fists across his head back and forth, over and over. He got a couple jabs in, which stung. But he was too caught off guard to fully defend himself. I was in a pure rage, unleashing every repressed emotion, every moment I sat and took punishment in silence. My fists connected with his face over and over. By the time the bus driver pulled us apart, I had a black eye, and his face was a gushing bloody mess.

I got home, and the bus driver informed my parents about the fight. I collapsed on the kitchen floor, sobbing. I had never felt so dirty and disgusting in my life. Violence felt monstrous, and I felt like I had become a monster. My dad congratulated me.

The next day, I was summoned to the principal's office. He played the security camera footage from the bus and watched it with me. I relived everything again, watching that video in the principal's office. I held my breath, waiting for the punishment: perhaps expulsion, or worse. The principal barely concealed his laughter at watching this scrawny, awkward kid flail his fists.

"Are you ever going to get in a fight again, Alex?" he asked, in a mock tone.

"No," I shook my head seriously.

"Okay, go back to class."

The other boy never came back to school again.

11

TOTAL WEIRDO

The next three chapters are my teenage experience of searching for love, told in three threads, each their own chapter: friendships, siblings, and finally romance.

When high school arrived, I was even more out of my depth. Class assignments and tests were easy for me, though. I never had to study, or even pay attention in class. I got straight As on everything. Instead, I focused all my energy on trying to gain acceptance socially. Remembering that play of *The Hobbit* from church fondly, I traded singing in chorus for acting in theater class.

As bad of a singer that I was, I was probably a worse actor. I could stand on stage, and deliver lines with a false bravado, but any amount of choreography left me a tangled mess, tripping over myself on stage. I was inept at even basic traversal across the stage, always missing the mark or the cue. I was given ensemble roles in the school productions: *Beauty and the Beast* and *The Wizard of Oz*. But mostly, I enjoyed theater because it allowed me to be among the goofs and the weirdos.

```
My brain is weird.
We were in Dance Rehearsal for Beauty & the
Beast
and everyone was wearing some sort of stripes,
plaid, checkers, etc. and it kept distracting
me.
Whenever I see a pattern, millions of math
equations start running through my head.
but the equations aren't made of numbers
they're made of colors, textures, light, place-
ment, size, etc....
```

```
and

its really annoying
but its a sort of automatic thing my head does.
I'm a total weirdo.
```

Alex, Age 15

I was often told I should sign up for football. "You have the build for it," people would say – even my dad. "You could be a linebacker." I was growing quickly, and turning from a scrawny, wiry kid into a tall young man. Even still, this advice made no sense to me. I felt incredibly small. I grew out my hair to hide behind it, and would walk while dragging my feet and hunching my shoulders.

```
Whenever I have a lot of things going on that I
COULD be depressed about, i start acting like
a 6 yr old; really hyper and happy and "jolly".
well, more than usual. but everyone gets mad at
me cause im really annoying. and theyd rather
be all serious and upset and wallow in their
misery.
so, should i give up?
should i just focus on my teenage angst, and
not concentrate on bigger and better things?
well. maybe i should just go around depressed
and wear all black. Of course thats not why
i wore all black today...that was a freak
accident.
anyway, thats not what im going to do. but,
whenever im genuinely happy, people are upset,
or having a bad day, and it brings me down. but
it only upsets me because i care about them.
so, please dont get mad at me. just tell me to
leave. Or ask me to be quiet. or just slap me
in the face, if you prefer....
whatever.
```

```
i try to be a happy person.
And i will continue to.
and when other people are concentrating on the

negative things, it makes me do it too.
and then i get upset and depressed.
trust me.
i have a horrible life too.
```

Alex, Age 15

During these high school years, I was confounded by a paradox of urges: the desperate need to hide, and the overwhelming desire to be seen. It was the early days of the social internet. I messaged people into the early morning hours on AOL Instant Messenger who hardly messaged back, I wrote vague and depressing life updates on Xanga, and I obsessed over making my MySpace page the ultimate symbol of my identity. MySpace was a simple website at the time, with boxes for you to put your likes, dreams, and rank your friends. You could customize the page with colors, fonts, and animations. Browsing through MySpace was a sea of dadaist and jarring visuals, each page crammed with ennui and pleas for validation.

I approached this how I approached many things: it was a puzzle to not just solve, but master. Remembering all the times I broke our family computer and my uncle fixed it, I taught myself how to break the web page. With some clever HTML and CSS, I blanked out the page and removed all the little predefined boxes for the user bio and content. In its place, I created an entirely custom page, meticulously designed to show off exactly how much my page did not look like anyone else's. It's thanks to MySpace, and my desperation to be special, that I learned web design. At the time though, I was only interested in using it to post melodramatic pleas for attention.

```
my parents make me angry. yesterday my parents
won some online shopping spree for 500 dollars.
so i walked around the mall with all my
siblings, while they sat in a store for 3 hours
for some timeshare thing. then we got home and
i logged on to use the computer to help my
parents use the online thing. i know how to use
```

computers. they dont. my mom think she does. but she doesnt. someone instant messaged me while i was helping my mom on tne computer. my mom threw her hands in the air, told me that the person should be able to wait a minute until my mom was done, and then she stomped out of the room. there is no way that person had any way of knowing i couldnt talk to her right then. then my mom gave me some crap about why dont people ever get up to go to the bathroom....why was she online....why didnt that person wait to message me until my mom was done...yah. like she was supposed to know not to message me. my mom was screaming and yelling for no reason, but as soon as my dad got home, she was calm and cool. i was the one screaming and yelling, she claimed. she said all she did was quietly ask me not to talk to my friends. yeah right. but who does my dad believe? her.

this morning my dad told me to go out nd help my bros clear tree limbs out of the yard. so i went out and helped. as soon as my dad left to go somewhere, my bros decided they were done. i told them that it wasnt finished, and they should come back outside. My brother decided he was going to be a jerk and scream and cuss at me, and say he just didnt want to do it, cuz dad wasnt here to make him. my dad came home, and i was still outside cleaning the yard. i told him what my bro did. but my dad yells at me. My brother helps him all the time....he cut the grass last weekend...he goes with him on weekends to work...yah. but i

```
dont do anything apparently. thats bullshit. he
thinks just because i dont do stuff he likes,
like pour concrete, and fix plumbing, i dont
do anything at all.

My mom screams at me, and twists everything
around, but then lies to my dad when he gets
home. My brothers act like an ass, but when dad
got home "he was planning to go outside in 2
minutes, but alex yelled at him". my parents
cuss. they lie. they are rude. they scream.
theyre always upset. they get pissed off at
everything. they grab me and throw me across
the room and shove my face into the ground. why
do they expect me to treat everyone else with
such kindness?
```

Alex, Age 15

There was another group of friends that I attached myself to, and grew close with. They all attended a bible study once a week, led by the mom of one of the girls. I started attending this bible study too. It was basic stuff: reading scripture, sharing stories, singing songs. It wasn't the Catholic rites I was used to – it was a more freeform, homebrewed version of Pentecostal. I didn't even know if they went to a church. It seemed to just be these kids, their mom, and some of her friends.

The mom announced that she would be leading an overnight retreat for us kids. I was happy to attend, and share a night away from home with these friends. It was seven of us teenagers, and three adults. It started off normal enough. There was journaling and games. We spent the night in bunk beds, chatting and gossiping.

The next day, we gathered in the main room and one of the adults had us sit in a circle. Then, she proceeded to use her "gift of prophecy" to pinpoint our greatest sins and insecurities. Already, I was skeptical. She closed her eyes, and began humming. The humming turned into babbling and chanting, and then she would announce something like "someone in this room has been struggling with pornography, who is it?" One of the boys would raise a hand, ashamedly. "Someone in this room wants to be accepted by their family but feels hated, who is it?" One of the girls raised her hand, with tears in her eyes.

This divination occurred for everyone in the room. She would highlight a vague point of shame, goad someone into associating themself with it, and then invite them to turn their heart to God to be free of it. When it came to me, it was something like "someone here is obsessed with stars and planets," and "you hate yourself." I suppose that's how they saw me.

Next, they informed us that we needed to be made free of our demons. We were told that demons took up residence in our bodies, and had to be exorcized with a ritual that only the adults were trained on how to do. They put on loud, intense music. We lined up, and one by one they laid hands on us. They were screaming and chanting in tongues, and infused each child with the power of the Holy Spirit by slapping them on the forehead. Each of them fell on their backs, screaming nonsensical words. One girl was frozen with her hands outstretched like a cross for hours, crying. Another vomited over and over, purging the demons. I was the last in line. They came to me, and chanted in my ears, loudly. I was ready, fully awaiting for the power to overtake me and change me into something better. I held my breath, allowing myself to exist in that limbo state between skepticism and allowing something magical to occur.

They slapped me on the forehead. I stood there, waiting. Nothing happened.

They did it again, harder this time. I waited for the divine energy to sear through me, and erupt out of my mouth in the language of angels. But, nothing happened.

After the ceremony, they assured me that it was okay that it didn't happen to me. They promised that it might work next time. I watched as people sobbed on the floor around me, overcome by the power of suggestion. I never returned to that bible study. I grew estranged from those friends just as quickly as I had attached myself to them, and looked for other people to make myself an accessory to.

```
I hate that I'm such an attention seeker.

i just hate myself, because im so annoying
and stupid and random, and people hate me for
it too...Like, today, (and most days) i was
sitting behind someone i know, and i kept poking
them with a pencil, and pulling on their hair,
```

and pinching them, and doing most things a little six year old would do.

and later today they were calling out numbers for scripts, and i said "Bingo!" because i thought, in my immaturity, that it was semi-funny. I was just trying to get attention, i guess... Everyone looked at me, and said "do you have that number?" and i said "no.... i just said bingo....i didnt mean anything" and they all said, "shut up, no one likes you. you dont have any friends, get out of here,."etc. And i know i shouldnt give a crap about what other people say, but its been a constant thing since kindergarten. I've being made fun of, for my looks, my smarts, etc. I constantly seek attention because subconciously i think, if someone isnt talking to me, they must hate me. thats my process of thought. its stupid. if you dont talk to me every five seconds, and im not the focus of your attention, you must hate me. its stupid, i know.i dont want to be like that. ive just been programmed that way since i was a kid. im trying to de-program myself.

If you walk by me to talk to one of your friends, i automatically think, "did i do something wrong? why didnt he/she stop to talk to me? they must hate me!" and then millions of absurd reasons of why someone would hate me run through my mind, all dealing with the way i look and the way i act. and then i start obsessing over those little things, like making sure i dont walk too fast, or i dont tell the wrong joke, or

my fingernails are cut perfectly, or i dont talk
too much, or i dont talk too little, etc. etc.
etc... I get this idea in my mind that someone
is always watching me, scrutinizing everything
i do or say, so i begin scrutinizing myself
and constantly being on guard. im constantly
playing with someones hair, writing on their
papers, interrupting them, just trying to get
someone to pay attention to me. I'm not really
trying to be selfish or be in the spotlight or
anything, its just a mental defense ive built
up since i was a kid. To pull my friends closer,
and constantly reassure myself, that there are
people who exist who actually want to be around
me.

I really dont know how to exactly explain how
my mind works.

And i know that other people have worse problems, and im not trying to be selfish and ramble
about my problems.

But i want to fix myself, and let go all of
those mental defenses and all those old ideas
about the way people are.

Until then,

please forgive me

for being me.

Alex, Age 15

I gained some small amount of confidence in my sophomore year – at least enough to tell a joke with the right timing and hope people laughed. I could put myself out there as a bit or a gag, and people tended to like it. That year, there was a Halloween costume contest, and I decided to enter – an opportunity for attention. Most people came with incredibly complex costumes, sewn by hand or made of many thrifted pieces. There were fairies, pirates, princesses, and dinosaurs. My costume, comparatively, was obnoxiously simple. I wore a black shirt, with a large letter 'P' made of felt and glued on the front. I painted around my eye with black paint.

I got to the contest, held in the theater as an after-school event. The place was packed. Cosplayers and would-be costume designers paraded across the stage, each getting a round of applause, and the judges made notes on each. Then, it was my turn. I walked up on stage, and approached the microphone.

"And what is your costume?" came the question.

I replied, "I'm a Black-Eyed P."

The place erupted in laughter. Moments later, much to the ire of the other contestants, I was crowned the winner of the contest. I felt quite guilty, as I upstaged the competitors who lovingly crafted their costumes with a cheap gag. I felt like I cheated my way into making people like me. But still, making people laugh was a rush. For a moment, the constant terror that I would be abandoned by everyone dissipated.

With some social credit earned from that event, I realized that I needed to move away from theater class. I still loved theater as an art form, but I wanted to be making, rather than just doing. The school had announced a new investment in a video broadcasting department, and I dove head first.

I quickly taught myself every aspect of it: operating the cameras, scripting, audio production and editing the videos. Editing was my favorite. With control over the pacing and timing of the cuts, you can manufacture emotion from raw footage – that was a power I adored. I became the head of the video broadcasting department, and produced reams of content for the school: the morning news, advertisements for school events, and hype videos for the football team's biggest rivalries.

I set up my schedule so my easiest classes were just before and after my video broadcasting timeslot, and negotiated with my teachers to skip class. I'd turn in math and history assignments weeks in advance, and get permitted to spend almost all day in the video lab, working. When it came time to do group projects for English or Science, I cajoled the teachers into letting me produce a video instead of writing a report. The other students loved this – much less work for them, and the result was exciting. I would write a script, cast my classmates in roles, and we'd all meet at the park and film a movie. Then I'd edit it, and we'd watch it in class.

```
So, today i felt..........calm.
not hyper or bouncy like usual.
What a change.
HMMMMMMMM.
I'm not sure wat to say.
dang look at those posts. i was depressed. well,
xanga isnt cool anymore. seeya
```
Alex, Age 16

I felt my brain changing. After entering public school with the social abilities of a fourth grader, I had to tap into some deep neuroplasticity. My junior year, I got my first Bs. It was a shock, and I didn't quite know how to feel. At the same time, I started developing confidence in little friendships: smiles in the hallway, shared jokes in the classroom. In one sense, my identity had always been "the smart kid who never had to study." On the other hand, it was like I traded some of the analytical and academic prowess for an ability to survive socially; to intuit the feelings of others, and make basic interpersonal connections. That was a trade I didn't know I was making, until it was made.

Senior year came around, and with it came "Senior Superlatives" – awards voted on by peers. I was surprised to be nominated for "Most Artistic." The class president liked me, mostly for those aforementioned video projects. She set up her table in the hallway of the school, and as the students came by to cast their votes for the various awards she gave instructions on exactly who to vote for. The award winners were set to be announced at the next big football game.

The stadium was packed. During halftime, the announcer rambled off the names, and students clambered out of the stands and walked onto the field to get their certificate and take a photo – "Most Fashionable," "Most Likely To Be President," "Funniest Student," and so on. I'm not sure if it was because of a thick southern drawl, a mistake in reading, or both, but the announcer called me onto the field as the "Most *Autistic*" senior student.

By the time the end of senior year came, I was truly enjoying high school. The kids would sit in the lunchroom segregated by niche – band kids, chorus kids, stoners, jocks, geeks – and I had friends at every table. I rotated through every group, making witty jokes or sharing plans for my next movie. Everyone knew me by name, though none were particularly strong bonds. I stood up straighter, and pushed the hair out of my eyes. It was like high school was a puzzle I had finally solved. It took four years, but it finally felt like I was ready to really *do* high school. I had the sense that if I was entering ninth grade at that time, I would have really been able to make the most of it – I would have been socially at the level my peers were at three years ago. And that's when it ended. It felt like I got six months of an experience everyone else got four years of, and I grieved over it.

12

COPING

While things at high school were steadily improving year after year, things at home were only getting worse. My coping mechanisms were unjustified hope, and total dissociation. A common refrain from my dad while he was barking at me was "why do you just sit there with that blank fuckin' stare?" But I was fully dissociated, mentally going somewhere else and numbing myself to the pain. To me, emotion was only pain. Feeling was just allowing myself to be hurt. Instead, I intellectualized everything, looking for the logic or reason to hold onto in an environment of chaos.

Still though, I was keenly aware of everything that was wrong in our house. I didn't feel, but I still labeled it as bad. In my teen years I got louder about it, defiantly insisting that "parents should not hit their children" and "don't tell us you are going to do something if it is a lie."

Every day, I'd get hit. I flinched when my dad walked behind me, bracing for a rough slap on the head and a degrading insult. Every day, I'd try to educate my mom on why children should not be hit, insulted, or told they are worthless. Every day, it accomplished nothing. Worse than nothing, it exacerbated the stress and anger in the house, and I'd get labeled as the perpetual instigator. Even still, every single day I'd go to bed believing that there was a chance that tomorrow, everything could change. Logically, it made no sense to believe that. The data clearly showed that things changing was not a reasonable expectation to have. Even still, that hope kept me alive.

I tried at every turn to connect with my siblings. Every day for years my brothers would run around the woods outside our house with airsoft guns, shooting plastic pellets at each other. They didn't wear any eye protection, but would often shoot from so far away that those little plastic bullets would rapidly lose all momentum before reaching the target. I didn't have any interest in this, but one day when I was about 15 years old I was feeling very lonely. I picked up one of their guns and tried to join the ruckus. I pumped the gun like I had seen them do many times before, pressurizing the chamber – 10, 20, 30 times.

I stood across the backyard from my next oldest brother, nearly a half-acre away. His back was turned. I looked down the sight and aimed for his head. I knew from this distance that the pellet would just glance off of his head, if it even reached him. And I had only ever shot a rifle once before, in Boy Scouts, so I figured the chance of me hitting the target was slim. I was excited to play their game, eager for them to grin at me wildly and chase me around the yard.

I fired. He stumbled forward, reaching around to grasp at his shoulder.

"Why did you do that?" he hollered, incredulously.

It took me a moment to realize what happened.

This wasn't an airsoft gun. This was a BB gun, with metal bullets – and it was absolutely dangerous, even at this distance. I didn't even know we had a BB gun.

My heart sank. I ran over to him. Defensively, I tried to make a joke out of it. He was stunned that I was stupid enough to shoot him with a BB gun. I was too. I took him into the kitchen and we examined the wound. Thankfully, it entered at an angle and was merely embedded in the skin. I pried it out with a butter knife, sheepishly put the bullet in his hand, apologized, and went to my room. What a stupid mistake. Far too stupid for a 15 year old to be making. I could have killed him.

I watched confusedly as my siblings got older, and they deeply internalized the abuse. Where I was stubbornly defiant, insisting that the situation was abusive, they seemed to accept it as a deserving reality. When I vocally protested the violence, our parents highlighted the protests as proof that I was the cause of division in the house – a lie that my siblings bought easily. I saw my mom doing nothing to stop my siblings from self-harming. I watched as my siblings would put themselves in terrifyingly risky situations with older people, and my parents chose denial instead.

I saw how the actions and inactions of my parents were setting my siblings up for self-destruction later in life, and I pleaded with them to do something about it. This went nowhere, so I internalized my own toxic identity as the savior and hero, and set about trying to save my siblings from my parents. I did this very, very poorly. I'd lock my siblings in rooms with me, trying to conduct some kind of intervention therapy. I was terrified they would spin out into a lifestyle of victimhood, self-hate, crime, or suicide, and was intent on preventing that. I felt that if I could protect them from the long-lasting effects of our parents, I'd be loved and accepted by my siblings. The desire for love and acceptance from my parents was something I had begun to let go of, but my siblings were a community I desired more than anything. However, they just hated me more, and understandably so. They were children, surviving my parents' dark kingdom in the only way they could.

I became deeply bitter and angry towards my mother. I was furious with her for the abuse that she enabled, and for all the times she assured us she'd make it better and never did. I began cursing at her frequently, telling her bluntly the ways she had irreparably harmed every member of the family. I would snidely call myself a "son of a bitch," and glare at her. She responded to this the way she responded to the pleading and the begging to stymie the abuse: a feigned gasp, and then denial.

This complex trauma affected me in deeply complex ways, but one more obvious and surface effect was the development of acute obsessive compulsive disorder. I became mentally chained to the concept of symmetry. As I walked, I would become obsessed with detecting whether I had stepped harder with one foot than the other. Then my next step would have to be harder on the other side to compensate. When I blinked, if I felt I blinked harder with one eye, I'd squeeze the other one tightly to create balance. I'd spasm my shoulders and jaw in rhythmic sequence, searching my body for a sense of relief and peace that never came.

Towards the end of high school, our dad checked out of the family even more. It was a steady stream of anger now, no longer punctuated by confusing moments of sentimentality. The bills piled up, and money was non-existent. Even with both parents working, every dollar was quickly converted into beer, which was quickly converted into violence. Christmas came one year, and my mom told me there would not be any presents.

This was unacceptable. Christmas Day was the one day a year we all looked forward to. It was a day where the impossible happened. And most importantly, it was a day I felt accepted by my siblings. I couldn't allow this to happen. Santa had to exist, even if it meant becoming Santa.

I created spreadsheets for each kid and what they wanted. I made sure it was equitable and fair, with a selfish eye towards toys and games I'd be able to connect with them over. I opened my first credit card, and ordered everything. I wrapped everything myself, kept it hidden, and crept out at two in the morning on Christmas to set everything up. Christmas morning came, and disaster was averted. Everyone opened their gifts, and had a nice time together. The debt didn't matter.

I did this for the next four Christmases.

13

A SEARCH FOR MEANING

Throughout high school, I attached myself to another of the girls from the Singing Trio – the funny one. Starved for any kind of affection, I harbored an extremely obvious crush. I orbited around her, constantly trying to anticipate her needs and make myself indispensable. We talked constantly, sharing countless inside jokes, and made our way through four years of high school attached at the hip, more or less.

Meanwhile, I got more involved at church. Our church was fairly contemporary, for that time and locale. It had a youthful energy, and there was quite a large contingent of families that stayed active in ministry with a focus on charity and service. The music was upbeat and modern with influences from the Charismatic and Renewal movements, and the attitudes of the clergy were much more pastoral than suppressive. Overall, I feel quite grateful to have been at this church with this particular flavor of Catholicism, especially considering how people in the Catholic Church have harmed, silenced, or shamed others. It is a privilege in my upbringing I don't take lightly, and one that certainly does not absolve the institution of the harm it has caused to many others.

As high school began, I was given two commandments by my parents, which are perhaps the best thing they ever did for me: attend the youth group, and volunteer at Mass. These would be transformative – not because of the rites and the liturgy, but because of the community I found there. So, I got involved with the youth group. They ran a program called Life Teen – a parish-based curriculum for high school students. As for volunteering at Mass, there were essentially two options: being an altar server up front, or being an usher in the back. I chose being an usher, and joined the ranks of the other kids with unmedicated ADHD in the back of the sanctuary. As an anxious kid, Mass was much more tolerable with the slew of side quests that ushering provided: spotting empty seats, passing out offering baskets, counting the bills and checks and placing them in a safe.

There, in the back of the Church, wearing an usher name tag and giggling with the rest of us, was Natalie.

Natalie was my age, but because of how our birthdays fell around the start of the school year and because I skipped a grade, she was two grades behind me. I was all-consumed with my crush at school, and Natalie had a toxic on-and-off-again boyfriend. We were not good friends at first: I pestered her quite a bit, with teasing jokes and stealthy taps on the shoulder. She found me very annoying.

In the youth group, the sacrament of Confirmation was approaching. As part of our preparation, we had to choose a weekend retreat to attend. There were a few options provided by the Archdiocese of Atlanta: a trip to the beach for leadership training, a weekend in the woods doing high-ropes courses and rock walls (Natalie's favorite), a weekend in the city building houses for the poor, or a weekend in a cabin listening to talks and journaling. I hated the beach, was scared of heights, and felt very intimidated by the thought of doing construction – so, I signed up for the quiet, reflective weekend.

The retreat was called Search. I arrived with a few teens from my parish, along with many others from across the state. We were divided into 'family' tables, and each table had an assigned pair of older students who acted as mentors. The weekend proceeded in the typical 'Cursillo' format: talks and testimonies from older teens and adults, games and activities, journaling, and ample time for reflection.

That weekend saved my life. I was 14, and Search arrived in my life at the moment I believed I didn't have much to live for. It was a religious retreat, but not one that focused on dogma or rules. Instead, the focus was community. It emphasized a perspective rooted in mysticism: we are all fundamentally and inextricably connected, and love is the greatest force in the universe. For teenagers who feel alone and astray, this is a powerful message. For me, perhaps even more so. The experience of spending a weekend with a 'family' that accepted me without condition, valued my words and feelings, and actually desired my company was a high I had never experienced before.

I've often met people who deride these retreat experiences as manipulation. These types of experiences are, of course, designed to manipulate. You're taken from normal life, deprived of sleep, bombarded with messages of struggle and triumph, and coaxed into being vulnerable and sharing yourself emotionally. It is no surprise, then, that by the end you feel deeply bonded to the other participants in a sense of catharsis. But all stories are manipulation – journeys that take you somewhere, if you let them. And that story, the story of belonging and being loved, was one I desperately needed to hear.

The weekend ended with a climactic surprise. We were led on a blindfolded walk. Holding hands with my new found-family, I listened as someone delivered a sermon on 'trust.' We were led through the woods, warning each other of roots and stones as we felt our way forward blindly. Then, we came to a halt.

"Open your eyes, and find your family," the leader said.

We all opened our eyes. The other attendees gasped – we were surrounded by familiar faces. Every teen's parents and families had come to close out the weekend. My parents and siblings came too, clapping along with the others. I think I was the only teenager disappointed in that moment, frustrated that the people who had deprived me of a sense of belonging for so long would intrude on this holy place. That they would trample on my new found-family.

Tearfully, each other teenager ran to their families, joyful that they were present to share in the closing of a powerful weekend. I hugged mine too, participating in the shared charade.

I attended every Search retreat for the next three years, and they were offered two or three times a year. It was addictive. After having attended as a new Searcher once, each subsequent time I was on 'staff'. I led many tribes of younger teens, being 'Dad' to many new Searchers. I grew in the mentor role, connecting with lots of other young people who had horrific home lives or struggled with various burdens. When she was eligible, I encouraged Natalie to attend Search as well. At the final trust walk, she opened her eyes and I was there along with her parents ready to hug her. She fell in love with it, and soon became a veteran of the event in her own right, helping evolve the format and stewarding an incredible community.

Back at school, I navigated my romantic feelings towards my friend extremely awkwardly. I summoned the courage to ask her to go to Prom with me. She said yes, but in the context of a group of us all going to Prom together as friends. There were some awkward attempts at dancing, and I waited for a slow song to come on to make my move. Every teen movie played in my head, as I waited for my chance to pull her in close. The DJ never played a slow song. The night ended.

Then, senior year was coming to a close, and the final summer before college was approaching. I was feeling a pull to finally make a grand romantic gesture to my friend, before time got away from us completely. We were a couple of dorks and hadn't dated anyone in all of high school. We attended a house party thrown by a mutual friend in their basement, and the anxious energy of an ending era filled the air. We played spin the bottle, but everyone in the circle chickened out of actually doing anything. As the party came to a close, I said my goodbyes, and headed up the stairs, hoping she'd follow. She didn't.

I then called out to her, voice cracking, "Will you come up here please?"

She came, meeting me halfway up the stairs.

I kissed her quickly, and awkwardly, stooping over her from several stairs up.

"Okay. Bye," I said. I left.

Several days later, we met at school. After a long conversation, we agreed to start dating. In part, we were doing so only because it felt inevitable. We had spent so much time together, and throughout high school I had latched onto her in an extremely fragile state and dysfunctionally made her my purpose in living. For her, I was comfortable, safe, and perhaps provided a shield from the embarrassment of entering college without ever having had a boyfriend.

At the same time, I was growing closer to Natalie. We had formed a small and close-knit friend group from church, and spent a lot of time chatting online and taking walks in the park.

The summer ended with a phone call from my girlfriend.

"Hey. We need to break up. We are going to college and it just doesn't make sense."

I cried that night. But in truth, by dating for three months, we realized how different we were. We had codependently leaned on each other as crutches to get through high school. But we did not want the same things out of each other, or out of life.

At some point, I stopped by her house to give her some things back. Then, once, we met at a coffee shop in an attempt to gain some closure, but it was awkward and ended quickly. We never spoke again after that.

My dissociation had been percolating throughout my high school era, and now it was coming to a boil. I was disconnected, like my life was just something that was happening to me. The passage of time and the whims of people around me were puzzles I could not master.

Heartbroken and feeling discarded, college began.

14

THORIN OAKENSHIELD

I thought I had to go to Georgia Tech. My uncles had gone there, and I wanted to be like them. But, I needed to apply to more than one school, just in case. In-state tuition came with a discount, so out-of-state schools were out of the question. I needed the public grants, so private colleges were not considered. The biggest deciding factor, though, was how my school selection might prop up my ego. I found that most public universities in Georgia accepted all applicants above a minimum threshold of criteria, set by the state. There were only three schools in the state that were permitted to be selective and choose applicants according to criteria above the state minimum: Georgia Tech, University of Georgia, and Georgia State University. I felt like those schools would cater more towards my identity as a "smart kid." I had an SAT score of 1980, and I applied to all three.

I got accepted by all three. I was proud that I was accepted by Georgia Tech, but started hearing many stories about how it was a "weed-out school" that intentionally made your classes as difficult as possible. I realized that I did not want school to be challenging – I wanted it to be easy so that I could maintain my image as a near-perfect student. I didn't want to go to the University of Georgia, as that is where my mom went. So, at 17, I enrolled at Georgia State University as a Computer Science major.

Georgia State was a university in downtown Atlanta without any proper campus. The buildings with classrooms and auditoriums were scattered across the downtown region, interspersed with office buildings. Instead of walking across a college campus, getting to class meant walking down busy city roads and dodging cars. There were few spaces for congregating and making friends, and none that I felt encouraged to occupy. I was still angry that high school had come to such an abrupt end, and frustrated that I had to start all over, socially.

One weekend, I went back home. Any space that could have been considered mine in the house was gone. My stacks of books had been donated. My box of legos was given away to some kid down the street. It felt like the moment I moved out, I had been erased.

Instead, I would spend weekends at a friend's house, and Natalie would too. We would share secrets, listen to music, and tell jokes. I sensed that I might be developing a crush, but I repressed it. It had become a meaningful friendship, and I didn't want to threaten it. Soon enough, though, we were hanging out as a duo, going to the mall just as an excuse to see each other. We'd walk hand-in-hand, refusing to interlace the fingers as if it was proof we harbored no feelings for each other.

On her 17th birthday, I visited her family, and we ate spaghetti. She got it all over her shirt. I didn't know it at the time, but she was as nervously smitten with me as I was of her.

One night, at midnight, she called me crying. I don't recall exactly what crisis was occurring – only that she was immensely distraught over something. She was spiraling, and overcome with feelings of worthlessness. It was raining hard that night. I got in my car and drove straight to her, engine sputtering in the storm. I got to her house, and she snuck outside to see me. We sat on the hill outside of her house at 1 AM in the downpour, just holding each other.

Then, on the morning of my 18th birthday, I woke up at our mutual friend's house, and she was there, staring at me. I kissed her. She kissed me back. Sheepishly, we spent some time with our mutual friends that day, and pretended like nothing happened.

Two days later, we met at a park.

"So, do you think we should date?" I asked.

"I would like to," she said, grinning.

I was worried about ruining another friendship. I believed that if she liked me, then I was somehow deceiving her. I was coercing her into caring about me through bravado, charm, and kindness.

I stared into her eyes. She was brilliant, and beautiful. It felt like she saw me, and it felt like she saw the world like I did – all full of boring rules and hidden adventures.

"What if it ruins our friendship?" I asked.

"It will make it better," Natalie said. She seemed extremely confident.

After a few dates, I was perusing some things in her house, and I saw a picture. It was a photo of the cast of *The Hobbit* – the play I was in as a child.

I seized it. "Why do you have this?" I asked, incredulously.

"I was in that play," she answered.

"I was in that play!" I exclaimed.

Sure enough, in the photo, was nine year old Natalie next to 10 year old Alex. The kind woman I remembered that helped me practice my lines was her mother. Natalie recounted that she remembered despising me at the time, because they reassigned her role to me after I joined the group. She had played Thorin Oakenshield in a prior community production, but they gave that role to me when I joined for the church play.

I went back to my dorm, and dug through a box of the few precious things I had kept from childhood. I pulled out the script of The Hobbit that I had kept for nearly a decade – the green folder given to me with another child's name in the corner eight years prior. Sure enough, there it was, scribbled in a child's handwriting: *Natalie*.

15

COVERED IN FLEAS

My mother announced she was providing our dad with an ultimatum – give up alcohol, or get a divorce. I was brought back from college to join the activities. There was a makeshift family intervention, and an official intervention with a family therapist. Each time, he stormed out cursing at us.

Then came the second time I've ever physically enacted violence on someone. I had come home for a weekend during college, and I was prepared to confront my dad one-on-one. He had been saying some particularly horrible things about me, and I wanted to plead with him once and for all to act with compassion towards his family. I had a speech planned.

He arrived, drunk.

I met him in the kitchen. "Dad, don't you see how you are hurting everyone?" I begged. "This isn't how a father that loves his family acts!"

In response to this, he became enraged, barking. "You think you're a big fuckin' man now, huh? You think you call the shots? I'll fuckin' knock you into next week." He lunged at me, and wrapped his hands around my neck.

In that moment I realized that I was a full head taller than him. I swung at him for the first time in my life, hitting him in the face. We grappled, I picked him up, and I slammed him down onto his back. He lay there, stunned, still cursing at me.

I got up. I walked away, shaking and crying. I felt his violence inside me, and I hated it. I felt dirty. I knew that if he stayed in my life, I'd only become more like him.

I never spoke to him again.

My mother, for once, kept her word and filed for divorce. My head spun. *Why had she done this mere months after I moved out? Why hadn't she done it years ago?*

Our dad spitefully kept the house, forcing our mom and my six siblings to move in with my granddad. I returned to college.

I was 18 years old now, and I felt coldly vulnerable. I realized that the prophetic vision from my mother that I had clung to was, of course, a fiction. Even if it had been true, that prophecy of me as an adult was no longer protecting me. It felt like I could be attacked from any side at any moment.

I started skipping classes. I saw other students with full, rewarding lives. They'd wake up, shower, go to classes, visit with friends, maintain extracurriculars, complete their homework, participate in hobbies, eat three full meals, and do it all again the next day. I did not understand how this was possible for them, or what was missing from me. I would arrive late at my first class, and then afterwards be so incredibly fatigued I'd return to bed for the rest of the day.

It was like a depressive, dissociative hibernation. For the first time, I had fully unplugged from my life at home and everything I had grown up with, and I didn't know who I was. My brain was emotionally and cognitively processing everything I'd ever experienced, leaving no bandwidth for even basic day-to-day tasks. It was a total shutdown. Most of this chapter of my life is a blur to me, and it clouded much of my memories of my childhood as I actively repressed everything. It has taken a long time since then to recollect the stories I've relayed here so far.

Natalie came to visit me when she could. These first few years of our relationship were somewhat long-distance, only seeing each other on weekends. She made sure I showered, and she took me to the store to get groceries for the week. I didn't know why she chose to do that for me, but there is no other word for it than love.

When I wasn't spending the weekend with Natalie or trying to attend a class, I was losing myself in Minecraft. Minecraft wasn't yet the global phenomenon it would become. At the time, it wasn't even released yet. It was in beta, and had a niche fanbase of nerdy college kids. I was a founding member of one of the original Minecraft servers, and instead of doing coursework I spent countless nights designing buildings and landscapes to make it a more inviting place for players. It wasn't originally designed as a multiplayer game, and the original code couldn't handle more than 10 players without crashing. The server team and I heavily modified it to host more than 100 players simultaneously, and some of the code I wrote for that ended up in the official release of Minecraft.

It was 2009, and I spent all of my time online, staring into the maw of loneliness and pit of anger. I saw the pipeline of content that swallows young men whole. Other young men who felt cast aside, who felt alien – plenty of echo chambers welcomed them, offering them deceptive life vests of racism and misogyny to hold onto. Attractive lies pulled young men in, casting blame on other groups wholesale for their lack of community. I saw how loneliness became hatred, and hatred encouraged violence. It was the kind of slippery slope tailor-made for someone like me. And that world feels relieving to enter, at first. It starts with a defense of humor – a pushback against perceived censorship and political correctness. "It's just a joke" becomes the vehicle that transmits misinformation, the target of the joke reduced to caricature. The caricature then becomes the entire discussion, increasingly blamed for all of the young man's ails. A young man who couldn't possibly believe that they, in all of their victimhood, could be ever rightly accused of causing harm.

Seeing that world has granted me a lot of empathy for the people it consumes. They are still responsible for their own harmful beliefs, of course. But I saw what I had, that they didn't – I had Natalie. I had scattered memories of people that loved me when my own family didn't. Plus, that world asks you to discard your empathy. It asks you to scapegoat other groups for your troubles. I had been a scapegoat too many times. I couldn't do that to anyone else. I stood on the edge of that pit, and turned away.

The school year came to an end, and I had a report card of nearly all Fs. I adopted more of my mother's signature denial, and enrolled in another year of classes. The student loan money was drying up, so I had to move out of the college dorm, and move back in with my mom.

Every single day I would get up, leave home, and pretend to go to college. Instead, I went to the local library, hid myself away in a corner, and read. That year, I read the entire *Ender Saga* in that library, and countless other books.

I did this for two and a half years: I took out student loans, hid away playing computer games and reading books, and paid for the privilege of failing classes I never attended.

Natalie had begun her first year at Kennesaw State University. She adapted well, made friends, and started attending the Catholic center on campus.

Then, one day, I woke up and I was different. The fog lifted, and suddenly the impossible was conceivable again. It was like a switch was flipped. I was able to look at my life from the outside, for a moment. I saw the choices I was making, like a needle stuck in a groove, scratching over and over.

I envisioned someone I called "Alternate Universe Alex." I imagined an alternate universe where I had been given what I deserved as a kid. A childhood forged in enrichment instead of violence, where I had not been taught to be afraid of anything less than perfection. A universe where I could take it for granted that I felt safe, connected, and capable. I imagined what choices Alternate Universe Alex would make, and how he would live his life. It would certainly be much different than mine.

Then I asked myself: *I may not have Alternate Universe Alex's past, but why does that mean I can't have his future? Why shouldn't I imagine what he would do, and then do that instead of whatever comes naturally to me? What comes naturally to me right now is surely a byproduct of terrible experiences that I didn't deserve.*

Perhaps my brain had finished processing what it needed to process. Perhaps the key was the belief that I didn't deserve the pains of my past, thus I didn't deserve the future it was leading to. Perhaps I had reached within and found a seed of hope or identity that had been buried below all the layers of shame and abuse. Maybe there was a sense of belonging planted by the Gorslines during those formative years, just briefly watered by the Search retreat, and carefully tended to by Natalie. Whatever it was, I had found it. I had done some sufficient amount of deprogramming. I was ready to try at life again. I felt ready to begin college.

This wasn't true healing, of course. This was a crutch that got me out of a ditch, but I was still angry and terrified. I found the strength to put on a new mask, but I didn't know at the time what I was suppressing.

In 2012 I reached out to my granddad to help me change my last name. I wanted the last name I was born with, my granddad's name: Gambon. The GMC Jimmy, my original vehicle from my uncle, had sputtered and given out finally, so I didn't have my own transportation. Granddad took me to the courthouse, helped me fill out the paperwork, and I appeared before a judge.

"State why you are requesting a name change."

I was nervous. I replied to the judge with my prepared statement. "'Gambon' was my last name at birth. My mother married in 1993 and I was adopted by her husband, and took his last name. They divorced, and I wish to revert to my original last name, inherited from my maternal grandfather."

"Approved."

My granddad then helped me buy a used car – a 1999 green Buick Regal that drove like a boat.

I enrolled at Kennesaw State, taking advantage of their clean slate GPA program, bringing over only my college credits earned in high school. I still owed a huge amount of student loans, but academically I was allowed to start as a freshman.

16

GETTING UP

My acute OCD was all but gone, overnight. I was excited to begin anew, and find community. I was especially excited to spend more time with Natalie. I changed my major from Computer Science to Information Systems, as I wanted a vocation that focused less on lines of code and more on helping people solve puzzles.

I got assigned a dorm, and connected with my new roommates. For a couple years, we tried our hardest to be friends. They were fun when they were sober, but their college experience was deeply devoted to getting drunk – and when they were drunk, they would pick fights with anyone who was around. I have never touched alcohol to this day – for obvious reasons. Addiction runs in our family, and it certainly has very negative associations for me. Part of it, too, is a control issue. I don't want my inhibitions to be lowered, or to have my personality warp under the influence.

My roommates didn't understand this. I was glad to be the designated driver, and participate in their drinking games with a glass of water. But anytime I refused a drink, I got slurred accusations of judging them and thinking I was better than them.

Even though those relationships didn't stand the test of time, I am grateful for what warmth they were able to show. Once, I was in a three bedroom dorm, and there were only two of us living there. We thought it would be great fun if we could unlock the third room for guests to use and for people to crash in after dorm parties – but it was locked.

I formulated a plan, and started solving the situation like a puzzle. A puzzle that could win me some admiration and loyalty. I got a vacuum cleaner, dental floss, and a piece of paper. That night's party was just getting started, and everyone watched as I started to work.

I attached a long piece of floss to the paper. I slid the paper through the crack at the top of the door frame. I fed the floss through, letting the paper slowly sink down the other side. After a couple of pulls, the paper popped out the bottom of the door frame. I removed the paper, and now I had a loop of floss going all the way around the door from top to bottom. I looped the vacuum cleaner's cord, and tied the bottom end of the floss to it. Pulling from the top, I fed the looped vacuum cleaner cord through the crack in the bottom of the door. Pulling the floss carefully, the vacuum cleaner cord slid under the door until I had it about halfway – level with the knob on the other side. With some jostling, I pulled the floss over until the vacuum cleaner cord was resting on the deadbolt on the other side. Then, with the cord sitting snug on the knob, I let go of the floss, and grabbed both ends of the looped cord. With a quick snap of the right side of the cord, it rotated the deadbolt and unlocked the door. I was a hero after that.

Roommates rotated in and out over the next couple years – all strange characters. One was a compulsive liar who would dig through our things looking for proof of conspiracy. Another did lines of cocaine nearly every day, and tried unsuccessfully to get me to join him. He would brag about how he had been attending parties at a particular global superstar's penthouse since he was young, engaging in what amounted to crimes against a minor – and he had pictures to corroborate his claims. A year after he moved out, he was tragically found dead in the parking deck of an Atlanta hotel – an apparent drug overdose.

Aside from navigating the friendships granted by the roommate lottery, I also got involved in the campus Catholic center. It was a haven for misfits, led by a theatrically eccentric priest with a lot of love for the student community. It was a place to rest between classes, to get a free lunch, or to meet up on a weeknight for snacks and board games.

I attended all my classes, and started getting stellar grades again. On a typical day, I'd wake up, go to my first class, and then go to the Catholic center for lunch. Then I'd alternate between afternoon classes and hanging out at the Catholic center. A big group of us from the Catholic center would go to The Commons – the university's award-winning cafeteria – for dinner. Then we'd go back to the Catholic center and play games, do homework, or play volleyball. It was an incredibly deep, warm community. Somehow, I became a leader. Where in high school I was awkward and shy, and at Georgia State I was withdrawn and dissociated, here I was charismatic. Bolstered by Natalie's support and validation, I began crafting a life I could be proud of.

Besides Natalie, there was only one other friendship that had persisted from my teenage era: Lauren. Lauren had been a fellow veteran of the Search retreats when we were teens, and we had stayed in sporadic contact. In the beginning of my time at Kennesaw State, Lauren called Natalie and me to tell us about a new Catholic retreat she went on. It was called "Awakening," and she billed it as "Search for college students." I was sold immediately.

Natalie and I attended Awakening soon after that. It was a three-day retreat format, similar to Search: family tables, talks, journaling, affirmations. It was something popularized in a Catholic community of Texas, and had been brought over by some young adults to the Archdiocese of Atlanta. Because of my prior experience of attending nearly a dozen Search retreats, attending my first Awakening wasn't deeply transformative for me. But, it filled the hole Search had left behind. It was a place of safety, and joy.

After the weekend, Natalie and I and the other Kennesaw State students who were there excitedly brought it back to the community at the Kennesaw State Catholic center, and urged everyone to attend the next one. Many of them did, and soon enough Kennesaw State became the de facto hub of Awakening in Georgia. The leaders of the original retreat were looking for more help in expanding the program, and a group of about eight of us would go on to lead over 18 Awakening retreats across the southeast. We would handle every aspect of the events: signups, food, venue, programming, music, and logistics for more than 100 attendees at a time.

The focus of the retreat was community. Merely by participating in the retreat – and truly, by merely existing – the members were shown how they are deeply connected and deeply loved. And Natalie and I built friendships that will last a lifetime. Even still, I craved reconnection with my siblings. They were my original community that I felt fractured from, and wanted to feel a part of again. I wanted to connect with them over something, so I cajoled them into attending Awakening as well. At one of these events, I had not only Natalie, but three of my siblings at the event at the same time. I stood there on that Sunday, with them in the same room as me. These cherished members of my real family, with all of our history of division and cruelty, had become part of my found-family. They shared this space with me, not just tolerating me, but grateful for me. And I was grateful for them. I broke down weeping.

One other event from this era would become a defining moment – the second supremely stupid gamble in my life that somehow didn't end in catastrophe. I bought Bitcoin in 2013. Bitcoin was immediately attractive to me when I discovered it in 2011; it was a complex, geeky algorithm with an anti-authoritarian bent. I didn't have much money, but after two years of studying it I mustered up 600 dollars and spent it on Bitcoin. It was all the money I had in the world. An objectively foolish gamble on an unproven asset, but one that would pay dividends.

Natalie and I built a core group of friends, and when we weren't traveling across the southeast to put on retreat weekends, we were playing board games. We would play board games that had six of us in one room for 10 hours, agonizing over strategic moves. We would play games where 30 people split up into two teams, bluffing and deceiving each other with outrageous characters.

My self-assigned role in the friend group was the curator. The voice in my head told me to always brace for abandonment, and stave it off as long as possible by being as useful as possible. I felt I had to constantly ensure that everyone was having the most optimized experience, whether it was a conversation, a meal, or a game. Some people looked to me as a leader, but I never really wanted to be a leader. I just felt like it was my job to make sure that everyone was having the best time possible at every moment, and nothing was unplanned for. Thus, I spent every extra cent I had on board games. The first one was Dominion. It is fun, of course, to gorge your nerd brain on strategic moves and devise optimal plays. But more than that, I felt like board games were my leverage to convince people to spend time with me. I amassed a large collection: first 10 games, then 25, then 100, then 250. I wanted to have a game in stock for every conceivable scenario, across any player count, time allotment, or style preference. That way, I would provide as much utility to my friends as possible.

I hated this about myself. I loved the games, and the parties, and the community. But I hated how manipulative it felt, like I was cheating people into caring about me. I didn't feel like a villain, but I felt like everyone saw me that way anyway. So I had to become machiavellian in order to survive, always listening for ways I could selfishly play the part of the hero, and tricking everyone into loving me.

Eventually, my brother Matthew – the third oldest – made his way to Kennesaw State, and became a leader in his own right of a new cohort of younger students. Natalie and I eventually moved out of our respective dorms as we finished up college, and rented a house along with my brother Matthew and some other friends.

I had precious few meaningful connections when I left high school. I had found my voice in some ways, but hadn't made bonds. After college, I had friends I treasured more than anything. They were family. They were a village.

17

MY BROTHER'S KEEPER

The next three chapters are the story of my twenties, told in three threads, each their own chapter: brotherhood, marriage, and work.

By 2014, my siblings were trying to move on from the divorce and the past hurt in their own ways. Three of them were in college, and three were still at home with our mom.

My mother called me, frantically. My youngest brother, David, had been expelled from high school at 14. "I don't know what to do," she said. "I'm going to send him to one of those camps for troubled teens."

David had been 'troubled' for a while, but not by anything inherently wrong with him. He was a brilliant, sensitive kid. As the youngest boy in our family, he lacked the perspective and outlets I had, lacked the bonds that our other brothers and sisters had with each other just due to birth order, and grew up in an especially violent era of our family. Desperate for community and acceptance, he found it with peers who offered him weed. That rapidly evolved into joyriding with local gang members much older than him, performing petty crimes and selling drugs.

Our mom wasn't equipped to account for the staggering number of pains and influences in our childhoods that might push someone down this path, and certainly wasn't capable of dealing with it at such a critical juncture. However, I couldn't allow David to be shipped away, excommunicated for the sin of being deprived of love that he deserved. So, I had a conversation with Natalie, and Natalie selflessly agreed that we would take him in.

I drove up to where they lived, and confronted David. "Come on, you're coming to live with us," I said.

The conversation escalated into negotiation which escalated into argument. We were outside in the backyard of our mom's rental house, and he was spiraling out of anger and shame.

"Maybe I'll just go live with my friends. Maybe I don't need any of you," he yelled.

I insisted once again. "Just come with us. Get a fresh start, we'll do an online high school and get your diploma, and you can have a future you deserve."

"You just want to control me. Fuck you." He turned and ran through the backyard, towards the back fence. But, he didn't run quickly. I could tell in that moment, he wanted to be fought for. He wanted someone to prove that he was worth keeping. I knew that feeling well.

I chased him, and caught him. I hugged him. And he wept.

"Will you come with us?" I asked again.

He nodded.

Natalie and I fostered David for the next three years. It was difficult. We did our best to provide him with the kind of environment he never had at home. We included him in our friend group, took him on trips with us, and involved him in a local youth group. I bought him a laptop, worked with him every day on online school assignments, and had many long conversations about what he wanted for himself and his future.

The first summer he stayed with us, after completing a semester of online school, I walked in on him packing his bags.

"Where are you going?" I asked incredulously.

"I'm going to live with dad," he said, flatly. "I can do my school work there, when it starts again."

I saw red, and this would be the third and final time I ever enacted violence on anyone.

I knew, of course, he was only going to live with our dad because there he would have full freedom to return to his old life of drugs and gang activity. I also knew that the promise of doing his school work there was a total lie. But more than anything, I was furious. Furious that he would dismiss my open and proven offer to provide him with a better life, and replace me with the very man that beat me as a child. I was trying to be a paternal figure to him that neither he nor I had, and he would trade me in for the father that deprived us both of that. He would abandon me, and run into the arms of the man that hurt not only me, but was responsible for the state of David's life at that point.

The rage came out of me. I screamed at him, and I don't even remember what I said. A part of me felt like *Oh, you want dad? You prefer him? Okay, I'll show you dad.*

I lunged at him. I grabbed him by the shoulders and picked him up. My hand slipped around his neck, and I threw him hard down onto the bed. His eyes went wide in terror.

Images of myself at 14 years old being grabbed and thrown across the room flashed in my mind.

I immediately backed up, reversing across the room. I stood with my back to the wall, ashamed and crying. I hated myself for doing that. I hated myself for allowing that anger and violence to surge forth, and that was the last time I ever allowed that.

I apologized to David. On David's part, I think he was able to see how much I cared. It came out in the toxic, violent way that we had all been taught, but in that moment it was the language we shared. He saw that I wanted better for him, and he agreed to stay.

Summers were still especially difficult, though. Without the obligation of school assignments, he pushed hard to be given as much freedom as possible and wanted to spend time with people from his old life. He would sneak out often, and had multiple periods of extended sobriety followed by relapse. I often knew where he went and who he was with, but I had to temper the instinct to lock him down. I didn't want him to harm himself, but I also couldn't control every action he took and stifle him. Instead, I made sure he knew there was more for him. I reminded him incessantly of what he wanted for himself, beyond the hole he was trying to fill. And still, he always came back home, willing to listen.

At the end of 2014 I began my Master's degree in Information Systems, and was working on campus. Natalie finished her degree in 2015, and began working full-time. It was at this time that Natalie and I adopted our dog. We had talked for a long time about our dream to have a Nova Scotia Duck Tolling Retriever: a friendly, energetic breed adept at swimming and ideal for families. We found a litter in Alabama that had puppies up for adoption. Normally they were bred for dog shows and competition, but there was at least one puppy that didn't have the proper symmetrical face coloring required for the breed standard. So, Natalie, David, and I drove to Alabama to adopt the puppy.

We named him Thorin, after the role that we shared in that play years ago. Thorin rode in David's lap the whole way home, scratching.

I got a job at Emory University as a graphic designer, and we all moved to Atlanta. Rent was expensive, so we leased a house with friends. It was Natalie, me, David, three other friends, and two dogs in the house. Split amongst all of us, rent was affordable – discounted by the fact that a train ran through the backyard twice a day. It would shake the house each time, but we got accustomed to it. We named the house Train Station, and my friends invested deeply in helping point David in the right direction.

Many more things happened with David in that era, but those are his stories to tell. Ultimately, he got his high school diploma. Then he turned 18, moved in with our brother

Matthew, and enrolled in college in the Fall of 2017. He didn't make it to his first class though. He panicked about his future, and vanished from Matthew's apartment. He rapidly adopted the trappings of his old life once again, and we didn't hear from him for months until we got a call from jail.

I had hoped his rock bottom was when he was 14, but it seems he needed to hit it once more to ensure he was actually ready to claim his new trajectory as his own.

In truth, he had gotten lucky. The trap house he was living in got raided, and he happened to not have a weapon on his person like he usually did at the time. He was only carrying a misdemeanor amount of drugs, so he couldn't be charged with a felony.

He pleaded to be bailed out of jail. I knew that if he was bailed out, he'd go straight back to that life. He was going through withdrawals, and his tearful begging over the phone to be bailed out was laced with a desperation to get another hit. I knew that voice – it wasn't David's, it was the addiction's. I counseled my mom and consulted with my siblings, warning them that David needed to stay in jail. My opinion was that he needed to go through withdrawal where there was no access to relapse, so he could begin a recovery program after withdrawals had subsided. This was an opportunity for David to get clean, not to go back to the street.

Days later, I got a call from another brother. "Hey Alex. Dad is bailing David out right now. He said no son of his is gonna rot in jail." I was livid. Here he was, meddling in painful affairs that he took no responsibility for, only to make them worse. I started frantically calling rehab places, trying to find a placement for David at the last minute.

Then, I left work early, and I raced to the jail to get there before my dad did. The bail money went through, and David was released. I intercepted him, and he got in my car.

He made some weak protests, but eventually agreed to go to rehab. He went to the recovery program, and he excelled. I was an anxious wreck for months, talking him through the process and watching him grow into a new sense of identity. He has since used his experiences to mentor and guide countless other young people who are as lost as he was. He is a testament to transformation, a force for good in the world, and I am indescribably proud of him.

18

TIME TO TRYON A RING

It was time. Natalie and I had been together for seven years. We had gone through college, led countless retreats together, adopted a dog, and cemented a lifelong community of friends. She was, and still is, my best friend, and the only person I can imagine facing life with.

I bought an engagement ring, and kept it hidden at my office at work for months. It was a central white sapphire, as Natalie had no interest in diamonds. The sapphire was between two red rubies – a reference to a longstanding refrain in our relationship that we were best friends first, and lovers second.

I booked a trip to New York in 2015 for a work event, and invited Natalie to come with me. I took her to Fort Tryon Park: the highest point of natural elevation in New York. I told her we would take pictures. I directed her to stand at the railing of an overlook, and practice looking pensive. I took some pictures, and then, with her back turned, I knelt down behind her. She turned around. Surrounded by gardens and overlooking the city, I asked her to marry me, and she said yes.

We were broke, and our parents didn't have enough money to put on a wedding. But, I had that Bitcoin stashed away. I sold my Bitcoin to pay for the wedding and honeymoon.

We were married on October 8th, 2016. As a wedding gift to Natalie, I got her a box. We had amassed a collection of trinkets from our long relationship – favors, love letters, pictures, concert tickets, souvenirs. These were crammed into a tin for a long time. As a celebration of our relationship, I got a box custom made that would be big enough to contain all of our lovely memorabilia. But, when it came time to pack the box, I could not find any of the things that should go in it. So instead, I put a new love letter, some socks, a white rose and two red roses, and some other balms and ointments for the new bride. As I had it delivered to her before the ceremony, her gift to me arrived. She had taken everything in the original tin, and assembled it into a beautiful scrapbook of our relationship. Hilariously, we'd later find out that the scrapbook did not fit into the new box.

The wedding reception was held at the top of Red Top Mountain, with a few quirks. Our first dance was *White Lines & Red Lights* by Between The Trees, which featured us bounding across the room akin to the joyous waltz from *The King And I*. Breakfast was served for dinner. Literal toast was served on platters during the toasts. We had pies instead of a traditional wedding cake. We elected to skip the garter belt and bouquet tosses. And finally, we had a rave. The lights were shut off, we gave everyone glow sticks, we turned on colorful projectors, and I queued up an hour-long dance mix that I had spent over a year creating.

I had always enjoyed the buzzy head rush that a well-constructed dance song provides. A build up, crescendo, a bass drop, maybe even a key change. But, I felt that when it comes to entertaining a crowd, there's always the one part of the song everyone is waiting for, and they are just waiting impatiently for that part. So, I cut together a mix of just the best parts of my favorite pop, dance, and house tracks, meticulously weaving them together into an endless onslaught of danceable mania.

The more introverted wedding guests huddled outside, chatting and playing yard games, while the rest of us hollered and tossed glow sticks wildly.

Natalie and I stayed in a hotel downtown and took a mini-moon weekend. The day after the wedding we went to her favorite place in the city: The Georgia Aquarium. She forgot to bring comfortable shoes, so we bought her the funniest fuzzy slippers we could find in the gift shop.

In December we celebrated our honeymoon at Disney World. Now, we are not exactly Disney adults. If we were to redo things today, Disney World would not be at the top of the list. But at the time, we were a pair of twenty-somethings with stunted childhoods, and being immersed in whimsy and the curated safety of a theme park sounded like a utopia – and it was.

Over the next few years, I invested what pocket change I could spare into Bitcoin, trying to replenish what I had spent on the wedding and honeymoon.

In 2019, we bought our first house. We had been splitting a rental with friends, and they decided it was time for them to buy a house. Even though Natalie and I weren't particularly financially prepared for this, that meant that we needed to buy a house too. Renting for another year on our own just didn't math out, especially with how property values were supposed to rise.

We looked all over metro Atlanta for neighborhoods that had decent schools and weren't too far from the city. We made a list of over 50 houses that were for sale, and spent a weekend in February driving through neighborhoods and moving houses either to the top or bottom of our list just based on the locations and the exteriors. Then on that Monday, Natalie saw a new house for sale. We called our realtor, and asked her to arrange a visit.

The house was owned by a family that had expected to live there for a long time. They took a standard 1970s home and completely opened the layout up, removing walls and putting in new structural support. They added a sunroom, put in quartz countertops in the kitchen, and generally took great care of the home. They had to move suddenly for family reasons. We put an offer down immediately.

We didn't have enough money for even a 3% down payment, which was the minimum required. I had the small amount of Bitcoin stashed away, but it still wouldn't have been nearly enough to matter. I had an obscene amount of debt: those Christmases I financed, credit cards maxed out to take care of my brother for four years, and piles of student loans.

So, I made an objectively stupid decision – the third moronic gamble that somehow did not end in absolute disaster. We worked with our mortgage servicer to take out a second mortgage on the house, before we even got the first. This is truly a dumb thing to do, and if I knew anyone doing the same thing I would warn them that they were taking an incredibly foolish risk. If anything happened to diminish the appraised value of the property, we would be underwater and owe more than the house was worth. But, we took the gamble, and the stupid gamble paid off. We got the keys in April of 2019. Property values rose, and we later refinanced to eliminate the second mortgage.

19

HATCHET JOB

In 2012, while getting my Bachelor of Information Systems, I started working at the Center for Excellence in Teaching and Learning; an office on the Kennesaw State University campus.

CETL developed and executed programming for educators to improve in their profession: daily lectures, weekend conferences, week-long writing retreats. I started as an Operations Manager, which was a catch-all title for making sure everything ran smoothly. The role eventually morphed into a more creative one, and I was charged with creating marketing materials, graphic design, web content, database management, and still generally ensuring that the events went off without a hitch. The office was a short walk from the campus Catholic center, and I still went over there for lunch when I could to visit friends.

In 2014 I nervously took my first plane ride. Natalie and I flew to Seattle so I could attend a work conference. My next plane ride was in 2015 when we flew to New York City, where I proposed.

I graduated from my Masters program in the summer of 2016. My boss at CETL felt it was necessary to kindly push me "out of the nest," and urged me to take my new degree and pursue greater employment elsewhere. In August of 2016 I started at Emory University's Business School as their Marketing Manager.

Under the auspices of the Marketing and Communications Director, I led the school in brand overhauls, website restructuring, and ultimately the establishment of a Design team, alongside Marketing and Communications. I enjoyed working with my colleagues at Emory, but after four years I was more than a little restless. I was confused about my professional identity, and felt like I didn't have a career track to count on. My degree was Information Systems, but my experience was in events and design. I did some freelance web design and coding, but really I wanted to be a writer. I was working in marketing, but really didn't enjoy it. I was a generalist, but the job market at the time was catered towards niche specialists.

In addition to that, higher education was starting to feel like a sinking ship I needed to either escape from, or resign myself to going down with. I was also disillusioned with the greediness of it all. I felt like a sleazy salesman, convincing rich kids that they needed an expensive MBA, while the purportedly non-profit school had an unspoken policy of never failing a paying student for any reason. I was looking for a life raft.

Then in 2020, cryptocurrency entered a huge bubble. The price of Bitcoin doubled its yearly low and was still climbing, and the entire sector saw a huge amount of energy, attention, and money pour in. I had been watching cryptocurrency closely, and excitedly. In nerd spaces online, Bitcoin was heralded as an innovation that would bring freedom to those that were oppressed by an exploitative financial system. According to the various idealists and early adopters of the technology, Bitcoin would be a new store of value unshackled from the clutches of Wall Street and greedy banks. The underlying blockchain technology, it was hoped, would improve privacy and democracy – giving the everyday citizen ownership of their medical records, or easy access to voting, for example.

I believed all of this. I still do, in a way. At least, I still believe that blockchain technology *could* have been a force for equality. But, I was naive. I thought that everyone had pure intentions. However, greed is a virus, and it wouldn't be long before the entire industry became a festering breeding ground for scams and pyramid schemes.

As the core technology grew in popularity, fads came and went. The latest craze in the crypto space at the time was "meme coins" – copycat cryptocurrencies that gave membership to a club. By holding the token, you were "in on the joke," rallying around a mascot or a concept. The earliest example that set the tone was "Dogecoin." It was created as a satire; a parody of Bitcoin. No one ever expected the price to increase meaningfully, just like how for years no one realistically expected Bitcoin to be a path to quick riches. Just as Bitcoin was a community that celebrated a shared ideal of a more equitable future, Dogecoin was a satirical club that celebrated internet culture and humor.

In early 2021, a flood of new meme coins appeared in the wake of Dogecoin's surprising success. One of these was "Elongate." Elongate was cheaply named after a joke made by billionaire Elon Musk on Twitter where he said, "If there's ever a scandal about me, *please* call it Elongate." This was swiftly rebuked by some who cited his illicit riches, inappropriate behavior, and misinformation campaigns as scandal enough already.

However, at the time Musk was mostly seen as an icon of innovation and was loved by internet culture.

The Elongate coin purported to set itself apart from other meme coins of the day by pledging profits to feeding the hungry, and this caught my eye. It had a stupid name, but it was putting charitable endeavor up front in their messaging. It captured something in the zeitgeist of that era that was special. I saw the potential of this new community, energized by a silly joke and adjacency to a polarizing public figure, and I wanted to be part of this movement to redirect capital towards charitable causes. The graphic design was messy, and I saw a major opportunity for polishing the brand. I was burnt out at my job, so I started knocking on virtual doors.

I was still naively enamored with Bitcoin philosophically, and I had blinders on. I saw it as a utopian opportunity for global equity, and I didn't see how the technologists and idealists were being supplanted by fraudsters who wanted to make personal gain at the expense of gambling addicts. I saw it as a risk, but merely as an entrepreneurial endeavor that could fizzle out, and I might find myself back at a desk job one day. That was a risk I was willing to take in order to be part of something meaningful. If I knew then what I know now about the nascent cryptocurrency industry and the corrupt dealings that would rapidly become standard practice in that space, I never would have touched it.

I introduced myself to the two developers of the project, and offered my services free of charge. The website and social media were sloppily thrown together, so I wanted to help them with visual design and web design. As I created designs for the project, I started realizing how poorly the entire project was set up. Random people had been given passwords to the social media profiles, and multiple loud voices had emerged in the project as self-styled figureheads of the community. It was a mess. No one knew who was in charge of what, and people's skills were not being used effectively. They needed organization. They needed a plan. So, I developed a business proposal and pitched it to them, and then I got to work.

I put out a survey to everyone involved in the project, asking for their self-reported skills and areas of contribution. Then I sorted everyone into teams, with the most experienced individuals as team leads, all reporting to the project founders. These people weren't put through any kind of typical hiring process. There were no background checks, and the 'talent pool' was just the people that had attached themselves to the project in its earliest days – a self-selected group of crypto enthusiasts. Then, I hosted the first town hall with all of the volunteers, and explained the core vision of the project: to make the biggest charitable impact possible, and put traditional charities to shame. Unlike regular charities that might have less than half of contributions go to actual impact, we intended to be highly efficient and have everything transparently recorded on the blockchain as the world's first crypto-based charitable fundraising community. In the new structure, I made it clear that I was merely acting as a structural advisor in this initial phase, and then afterwards I would simply be on the design team.

It was a hit. Everyone was excited to feel like they were part of something official. But what I didn't know was that I was being set up as a patsy.

In the days that followed, we developed a concept for community livestreams. We would gather the community together for giveaways and games, and dramatically reveal our first huge donation to a charity. I asked for a volunteer to host the live event.

Silence.

Even the two founders declined to do this.

"Well," I said. "I guess I can do it just for the first one."

I should not have done that.

The event went well, but I was quickly affixed as the face of the community – the singular public persona amid a gaggle of aliases and online handles. One livestream to 40 people became twice-weekly livestreams to 5000 people. I was suddenly catapulted to micro-niche stardom, and I hated it. But, I wanted to see the project succeed. I saw how people were blindly throwing money at these crypto tokens, hoping for a chance to get rich, and I thought, "why not leverage that to actually do something good in the world?" But there were many in the project who wanted the opposite. They wanted to leverage the appearance of benevolence to part investors with their money. While I worked on web designs and charity relations, these "community leaders" spent hours each day on the voice chats, promising riches to all who would listen.

I saw the lighthearted humor of Dogecoin, and hoped to marry that with a real, sustained impact that we could be proud of. I didn't know how ugly it would get.

The community exploded to hundreds of thousands of members, and as word spread the money for charity poured in. We started donating hundreds of thousands of dollars weekly to charities. I hosted a revolving door of charity CEOs on the livestream, amplifying their message to our community, and unveiling massive checks from the community to those in need. I appeared on a talk show on the Lifetime network with one of our charity partners to talk about using technology to make real-world impact.

I flew to Miami to exhibit our company at the Bitcoin Conference. There I met several of the members of the volunteer community who goaded me into doing various farcical interviews with their favorite niche youtubers, appearing in videos with them, or who pitched their latest get-rich-quick scheme to me hoping to secure me as an ambassador.

Then the founders vanished, right as the project had inflated to unmanageable size. Instead of staying lean like a proper startup, we chased ever-expanding community expectations, fueled by the toxic voices on the group chats that were amassing a cult following. My time was full with doing livestreams, improving the website, communicating with charities, and writing press releases, so we quickly restructured to put people in charge of key areas: HR, Technology, Marketing, Community, Finance, and Legal. I took charge of the realm of "Storytelling," comprising both the digital events and partner relations. The people assigned to oversee the other functions hid behind pseudonyms, claiming to have the skills needed to help keep the ship afloat. I did not manage these areas at all, and merely hoped that the people who stepped up to oversee them would have altruistic goals. Without central leadership this was a doomed effort. I was held publicly responsible for everything to do with the project, but did not have the power to make it happen. I was the face of the company, but had no knowledge of most things happening behind the scenes, foolishly placing blind trust in a shared mission. People started getting paid small salaries: mine was exactly replacing my previous salary at Emory. I finally quit my previous job, and committed to working for Elongate, hoping that with increased focus I could right the ship.

It was a comedy of equal parts incompetence and malice. Later, the truth of these people would come out. The Head of Finance was funneling money to his friends for 'marketing' efforts. The Head of Marketing commissioned a massive global billboard campaign with no quality control, so billboards appeared for mere hours over slums and then vanished. The Head of Legal turned out to be a law student who fraudulently structured employment contracts to give his friends unlawful ownership of company IP. The head of HR baselessly claimed the title of CEO, and teamed up with the head of Community to stage a smear campaign against me specifically, fabricating claims of awful behavior. They stonewalled hiring efforts, and pushed through their friends without any additional approvals. The head of HR, it turned out, was a repeat scammer, who had past lives selling various kinds of snake oils.

I didn't know any of that, though, until the very end of things. All I knew at first was that company meetings were fraught with the other members making bizarre accusations, demanding more money and exaggerated titles, and urging everyone to artificially in-flate the price of the coin. Meanwhile, I was trying to maintain our optics and develop relationships with charities. People would gossip between meetings, and battlefronts of power would tug back and forth, childishly changing passwords or whispering to the community about who they despised. The only one of any real value was the head of Tech – a sensible guy with plenty of real-world leadership experience. I didn't hire any of these people, and I didn't have the authority to fire them. No one had authority over anyone else.

I was in over my head. This machine was spinning along at a million miles an hour, but from the outside everyone only knew me. They knew my real name, and where I lived. Everyone else was anonymous. I felt like not only my reputation, but my safety was on the line. At the same time, the rose-colored glasses started to slip, and I began seeing how nearly every other cryptocurrency project in that space was effectively a pyramid scheme. It feels obvious, in retrospect. I dug my heels in though, determined to be the example of nobility and honesty in a sea of manipulation. So, I did the only thing I knew how to do – I tried to solve it like a puzzle. I tripled down, working 19 hour days, seven days a week. The pandemic was already isolating, but this was a new level. I ignored my wife and all my friends for over a year, and I did nothing but wake up at 7 AM and work until 2 AM every day. I threw myself into a dark pit again.

We felt the pressure to make a bigger splash every time we donated to a charity. So, we reached out to a particular billionaire's brother. A billionaire in his own right, this brother ran a high-profile charity, and his celebrity status would satiate the community that wanted something exciting.

With the promise of a check of over half a million dollars, he agreed to appear on our livestream. This was a seminal event, and the community was practically frothing at the buzz his appearance could bring. It went as well as could be expected – he appeared, congratulated us on our accomplishments, thanked us for the check, and left.

Then, he asked for a private meeting with me and our head of Tech. We were tentatively excited – this could herald a new partnership at a high level, and give us legitimacy on top of our nearly three million dollars donated so far. In the meeting, he asked the last thing we expected: he asked us to explain how crypto worked. We proceeded to give him an hour-long private seminar on exactly what blockchain was, and how the technology operated. He then asked us to outline our business model, and how the charity mechanism functioned. Then he curtly said "thanks," and ended the meeting.

We were bewildered. Why would a man with his level of access need us to give him a primer on how the tech worked? Did he want to know about our business so we could work together?

A week later, we received an email from his office instructing us to never contact him again. The next day, he announced, to much fanfare, his new 'first-of-its-kind' crypto-based charity community. Ouch.

I was sent to Dubai in October of 2021 for two weeks of back-to-back industry conferences, and Natalie came with me – my first trip outside of the country, and nearly on the opposite side of the globe. I was trying to do what I knew to salvage a sinking ship. I gave two keynote speeches on our vision for the future of social impact, we exhibited our new technology for social fundraising, and met with other rising stars of the industry. We won the award for best social impact project. In between busy days of managing the exhibition, Natalie and I explored the city and attended the World Expo.

Then the bubble burst.

Bitcoin fell off a cliff, and took everything with it. In a bubble, you can throw money at anything and feel like a genius, because everything is going up. When the market receded, it didn't matter what influencers, charities, or journalists we worked with. It didn't matter what conference we went to, or how many livestreams we did. The price crashed, and I was held personally responsible by thousands.

I got endless death threats. People sent me images of my face that had been photoshopped to appear riddled with bullets. I lurked in chat rooms where people discussed what they'd do to my wife if they decided to come to my house, egged on by my fellow employees who I considered my friends. I labored under this treatment from the community and my colleagues for a long time, mostly because I felt I had no real authority to do anything about it. This triggered feelings from my childhood – scapegoated by my parents, who manipulated my siblings to perceive me as a villain. But still, I felt trapped. I couldn't leave, as my name was now synonymous with the project.

Bitcoin just kept tumbling.

In the end, the head of Tech and I painstakingly excised all of the toxic volunteers and employees, who each did their best to burn down the house on their way out. One even went so far as to create faked invoices that purported to prove that I stole money from the accounts. Another deleted troves of data as they left. They created narratives that I was a greedy, power-hungry diva who craved all the attention, stole all the money, and drove the project into the ground to spite everyone. They spread stories that I ruled the company with an iron fist, and projected all of their behavior onto me.

Finally, the head of Tech was able to actually look at the accounts and piece everything together retroactively. He discovered that the founders, as they exited, took nearly a million dollars of the community's money with them. We spun down the company, reduced to just core staff, and we stopped taking our salaries.

I was more than distraught. All I had wanted was to be part of something that made a positive impact. I ended up becoming the face of a crypto project that crashed, and was on the receiving end of death threats and libel manufactured purely out of spite, from a community that I had naively assumed to be altruistic idealists. In short, I had been very stupid.

Even still, we did make real impact. Under my leadership, we donated 3.7 million dollars to places that really needed it, especially in the wake of the pandemic. We spent $825,000 on food, clothes, and essentials for international communities besieged by war and famine, putting teams of volunteers on the ground there. We spent $800,000 on feeding urban populations in food deserts, we pulled $400,000 of garbage out of the ocean, gave $350,000 to create programming designed to lift children out of poverty, and donated $300,000 to build services that give young people with autism opportunities to live and work independently. We gave $200,000 to rare disease research, $200,000 to pandemic relief, and $150,000 to the treatment of kidney disease. We built a school in Laos, brought Christmas presents to underserved children in Los Angeles, and renovated a children's hospital in Orlando. I am immensely proud of that.

In spring of 2022, I stepped back from full-time efforts there, and looked for employment elsewhere. The head of Tech continued stewarding the project, building useful utilities and websites for holders of the coin. He still tinkers with it, using it as a testing ground for tech demos and entrepreneurial ideas. He calls me up every month or so to get my perspective on his latest inventions, operating it like a proper tech startup.

I leveraged my experience in blockchain and got a job with an international startup. The company was billed as a retail storefront with tokenized fashion products – an interesting use case for the blockchain, and certainly one that provides more real-world value to the consumer beyond just a virtual currency and feel-good donations.

When I joined, lots of promises were made. I was told that the team was currently in Korea, but their headquarters was moving to the US imminently. I was given a compensation offer that had a pretty small base salary, but a staggeringly large bonus structure. I was told that they needed fresh ideas and a western perspective to bring their technology to a wider market. I was told that employment contracts were coming soon, just as soon as legal issues were ironed out with the parent company.

I spent the next four months overhauling all of their collateral. I transformed their website, documentation, and internal messaging guidelines and brought them up to a high level of quality. I even traveled with the team to a week-long conference, taking on the responsibility of planning and executing our exhibition and writing the CEO's script for his speech. Meanwhile, I was periodically checking in with the CEO to see if I was performing to expectations, and was told over and over that I was impressively exceeding expectations. I was also assured that those employment contracts were coming any day. I foolishly continued working without a contract, motivated by the promises of a bonus nearly six times my base salary.

Then it came time for the first performance review, and the first bonus payout. I was finishing up a major marketing project, and they kept pushing back the review, citing scheduling issues, and withholding my pay until the review was finished. Wanting to be a team player and understanding of the hazards of a startup, I just kept working. Finally, I finished the project, and deployed a full year's worth of marketing automations, providing their social media and website with a detailed calendar of tailored content.

The next day, I was fired, without the bonus payout. On the same day, the other Americans who had been hired at the same time were fired too. On the call, they assured me that my work was up to par, but I merely wasn't a "cultural fit."

My best guess is that they wanted professional quality work, and dangled false promises of executive roles and big bonuses to get 4 months of crunch work out of us, to then leave us in the dust and springboard off of our work. Shameful behavior.

So, there I was. Stolen from, used, and gaslit. I was burnt out and distrustful of the world around me. Meanwhile, someone from my past was in the background, hovering on the edges, and things were about to come to a head.

20

BIO DAD

Growing up, I always knew I had a biological father out there somewhere. He was like an alien ancestor from another planet – the nameless proof of my extraterrestrial origins. When I got older and money was tight, I'd occasionally drift off in thought, wondering if he was actually a wealthy prince who would suddenly die one day and leave me a fortune. But I never really had a strong desire to meet him.

Even still, I was searching for a sense of identity. I wanted to be rooted in something – to have come *from* something. All I knew was that I wasn't supposed to exist. In fact, it seemed *wrong* for me to exist. I only came into being as the byproduct of a loveless act between two lost souls. That wasn't how people were meant to be made, I thought. But, perhaps knowing more about my ancestry would give me a sense of place. A sense of connectedness to what came before. So, in 2014, I did 23andMe genetic testing.

The test revealed nothing too unexpected: Irish ancestry, sensitivity to caffeine, elevated risk for Alzheimer's. I let the account sit for a long time.

A month before our wedding, a message appeared.

```
Sep 6 2016 | From R
Hi Alexander, I hope you are doing well! As you
can see, it looks like we are first cousins and
I'm just wondering if you know anything about
how this happened? According to my family tree,
I wasn't aware of another cousin. Just looking
to fill in some gaps, I'm intrigued!
```

I think I had a panic attack.

To R
That is interesting! I would love to find out
how we are connected. Are you in the US? Do you
have aunts/uncles in Georgia?

From R
I wouldn't be surprised if we were second
cousins but I'm a little confused as it lists us
as first cousins. To my knowledge, my father,
Q, has two brothers; M and C. I am unaware of
any family living in Georgia.

I shoved this to the back of my mind and focused on the wedding. It was six months before I got the courage to reach out to my biological father. I messaged him on Facebook.

Mar 24 2017 | To M
Hi M, My name is Alex, and I am 26 years old.
I have recently discovered that you are my
biological father. I am reaching out to you
because there is half of my ancestry that I
know nothing about. I am specifically hoping
that you can provide information regarding
any medical details, health issues, hereditary
conditions, etc. from your side that I would
need to know about. I'm interested in learning
more about my genetic ancestry, along with any
information you might think pertinent.

Mar 26 2017 | From M
Alex, you caught me completely by surprise this

afternoon. I knew it was possible that I had
fathered a child in my past, but I had no idea
how to verify that as I did not remember the
mother's name. Please verify that what you say
is true by telling me how your mother came
to know me and I would love to continue our
conversation.

To M
To my knowledge, you met while she was a student
at UGA in Athens, GA. This would have been
approximately January 1990.

From M
Did she say how we met?

From M
Hello?

From M
Just FYI... I believe that you are who you say
you are... you look like me and I believe Athens
GA was where we met... but just want to be
careful... I will tell you that I have looked
for you for many years and without knowing her
name, it was impossible... I searched ancestry
looking for anybody looking for me and could
never find it. I just prayed that someday my son

or daughter would find me because I knew that
their mother probably knew my name because of a
phone call I received back in the day from her
stating I was the father of an unborn child but
she did not assume/demand that I have anything
to do with it. Being the total reprobate that I
was, I quickly forgot her name and went on with
my life of partying and such... it wasn't until
I matured and my views of the world changed
that this came to matter to me. I would love
to provide you with any information you wish
to have.

I was so afraid of how this would go. In the moment, though, I didn't understand why I was afraid. I wanted it to be simple, and clinical. I wanted to say hello from a distance, and acknowledge each other for our shared genetics.

To M
I'm waiting for her to reply regarding those
details. I understand wanting to be careful.
The reason I was able to contact you is
because I am signed up for a service called
23andMe. This service has ancestry information.
I already knew your name, and via 23andMe I was
alerted that R is my 1st cousin. R contacted
me and told me that her father is Q, and Q has
two brothers - C and M. At that point I knew
I had found you. I did not tell R any details
about how we are related though, beyond what
the site says. I will let you know what my mom
says to confirm the story for you.

```
From M
By the way, your biological grandfather is
quite an amazing man. there is a park in France
named after him because of what he did in that
place...
```

This was a strange reply. He needed assurances, but was already telling me about distant relatives and family lore.

```
To M
Thanks for sharing that. I will take a look
later on.
```

```
To M
My mom just got in touch with me. The story
goes she met you at Athens Mall, and you were
selling magazines. You invited her to meet you
at the Holiday Inn Express near the 85/285
interchange. It was a one-night thing.
```

It felt so bizarre to type that. A strange inversion, to have to tell my biological father the story of how he conceived me.

```
From M
Yes... and sorry for such a bad story.
I did request you as a friend on Facebook and
then removed it... thinking that it should be
your request and not mine.
```

I did not want to be friends. Not yet. I wanted information. I had finally found the keeper of secrets – the person who held knowledge about me I never had access to.

To M
Let me know if you're able to provide any
hereditary/medical information. Do you know
your ancestry? 23andMe indicated that I have
Dutch and Irish ancestry, but I'm not sure which
side they come from.

From M
Well, we were adopted by our father who married
our bio mom... and I have twin brothers in Texas
and some sisters I have never met. I will send a
link to our ancestry family tree... I am 50 and
we have a family history of HTN and diabetes…
Let me know how I can help in any other way and
it was a pleasure meeting you.

To M
I appreciate you being so open to speaking with
me. Is there anything else I should know from
your genetic side? Any mental health issues?

From M
no... nothing mental... but if I think of
something I will send it your way.

I was disappointed, in a way. Hypertension, diabetes. That's it. Nothing revelatory. No new insight into who I am or where I come from.

```
To M
Thanks. I would love to learn more if you
think of anything. I appreciate you offering
the Facebook friend request - I just think I'm
not ready to make that level of connection.
```

```
From M
Understood... here is a picture of an article of
your great grandfather from a France memorial.
You can email me if you need to converse in a
longer format.
```

I didn't know what to say in reply. Becoming friends on Facebook seemed horrifying. The idea of scrolling through social media and seeing the face of my biological father in a sea of miscellaneous acquaintances was revolting to me, like it trivialized my entire life. My progenitor, the man who launched the arc of my life, should not be cataloged with former colleagues and college friends.

I sent a message to the cousin, letting them know the truth.

```
Mar 28 2017 | To R
I want to apologize for not replying 5 months
ago. This might come as a shock to you, but we
are indeed first cousins - M is my biological
father. I never knew exactly who my biological
father was, or how to find him - I only knew his
name. When you contacted me I knew that this
was it. I just wasn't ready to make contact
yet. However, I have recently messaged M and
we have been in contact. So, I just wanted to
say thank you. You helped solve a mystery that
I wouldn't have otherwise been able to solve.
```

```
From R
Wow that is crazy. I had no idea, M and I are
not very close at all. In fact, I'm pretty sure
I haven't spoken to him in over 10 years but
none of our family has heard about his having
children outside of his current marriage. I
won't mention this to anyone just to respect
your guys's privacy but I'm shocked! Good luck
with everything!
```

The lack of contact struck me. What had happened here? What caused a rift in their family? I didn't want to find out, but I was unnerved.

Nearly a year passed before M spoke to me again.

```
Jan 4, 2018 | From M
I hope all is well... I hope someday we can
get to know each other just a little bit more
outside of genetics... take care.
```

He was putting the ball in my court. In a way, that was appreciated. But this old man was a stranger. I inherited DNA from him, but I didn't know why that meant I should pursue a friendship. The life I had constructed in my twenties was built on a bedrock of found-family. DNA didn't equate to relationship, in my view. At least not merely by virtue of it.

The 'someday' he mentioned didn't feel like it had arrived. I didn't reply.

21

A SWEET OLD LADY

M ore than a year later, someone new messaged me.

Mar 18 2019 | From E
I'm your grandma - I'm so sorry I missed your
life.

I was shaken. This was M's mother. How had she gotten my contact information? What had happened suddenly, that she'd message me? What did she want?

To E
Hi there. Nice to meet you.

From E
My granddaughter found you through a DNA site &
my son Q sent me your pics. I was blown away!!!
I do not communicate w M, Q's brother & was not
learned of you by him. I am overwhelmed by you &
saddened that I missed your life. I'm wondering
if I have a great grandchild as of your recent
marriage? I would love to be a part of your
life, at least on line, from here on out? I am
76 yrs old & live in a self-serving retirement
center in Spokane. I have 10 grandchildren,

```
including you. Thank you for answering back &
I already love you! Grandma
```

My pictures were being traded among their family like Pokémon cards. I didn't like the assertion that my eventual child would be her grandchild, but I wanted to be polite to an old lady.

```
To E
It is totally okay! I always knew that I
had some relatives somewhere out there, but I
didn't know where they were. I spoke to M for
the first time two years ago. I am 28. My wife
Natalie and I have been married for 2.5 years.
No kids just yet, but maybe soon. We live in
Atlanta.
```

```
From E
I will be looking on Facebook daily for you.
Q & family are on Facebook too. He is in your
line of work too. I hope your life has been a
good one—just wish I had been in on it. Keep
me posted, please.
```

```
To E
I don't post updates on Facebook very often
unfortunately. My account hasn't been updated
in several years. But I can share a recent photo
with you.
```

```
From E
Beautiful photo of both of you. Your face says
you have a beautiful soul! I hope there is
someway that I can see your life from now on?
I will get that pic printed. Love, Grams
```

This felt out of control, but I didn't know what to do. Pictures of me were being hung in a stranger's home. Still, I wanted to be polite.

```
To E
The latest with us is that we have just bought
a house. I am a Designer for a University in
Atlanta. Natalie is a personnel director for a
company that provides elderly home care.
```

```
Mar 20 2019 | From E
This is all so bittersweet to me. Q, who travels
all over the world, tells me that when GA is on
his list, he would love to meet you! I can't
travel anymore because of Polio that I had when
10 yrs. It comes back, much worse, w age. No
one could tell I had it till I reached 57 yrs.
Q & 3 of his kids were just here visiting. I
have one son by late husband that lives here
in Spokane (C). Anyway, you have a lot more
relatives now! Grams
```

She seemed intent on telling me everything about her family. So, I asked her to tell me about my biological father.

```
To E
So sorry to hear about your Polio. That must be
```

very difficult. What is my biological father
like? M?

From E
Want to tell you about your grandpa—They named
a park in Fremonville France after him. There
is a dedication every 10 yrs, it seems. He was
in WW11 & the Cross of Lorraine signifies his
plaque there.

It seemed like she missed my question. I asked again.

To E
That's impressive! What can you tell me about
M and his family? Do you speak with them?

From E
He has 3 adopted children & married. No, I've
given up—it never ends well. There comes a time
when it's time to quit. I would not like to
talk about him to you & Q asked me not to do
so either. He, Q & family don't communicate w
him either but C does. I hope this doesn't put
a damper on our relationship? I'm so sorry & I
know it must be hard for you. I know what it
is like not to have known your father. My kids
had a wonderful stepfather, but I was not so
blessed. I made it tho! My dad was killed in
war & I never knew him.

This was strange. The rifts in their family seemed messy, and I didn't want any part of it.

```
To E
I understand, that doesn't have to be a topic
of conversation. I just don't know what the
situation is. I have only spoken to him briefly
in order to understand any medical history. But
yes I understand that family relationships can
be impossible. My stepfather was not a good
man, and we don't speak now either.
```

```
Mar 25 2019 | From E
Hi grandson! M's response to your phone call,
or lack thereof, upset me greatly! I just got
out of hospital w acute bronchitis & a bad case
of viral flu. Emotions make you ill that is for
sure. What a loss I feel by not having see you
grow up! Anyway, please keep in touch w notes
& pics. Here's my number if you wish to text.
```

M and I had never had a phone call. She seemed confused. I didn't reply.

```
Mar 25 2019
M would like to join your LinkedIn network.
```

```
Mar 27 2019 | From Q
Hello, nephew. I'm sure, by now, you might be a
little tired of us coming out of the woodwork.
Just thought I'd reach out and say hello! You're
welcome to reach out any time you like if you
```

want to learn anything about this side of the
family or just say hi. Warm regards.

To Q
Hello. It's certainly surreal! I don't think
there's anything I specifically know to ask
about right now. Thanks for reaching out.

Apr 2 2019
M invited you to connect on LinkedIn. His
invitation is waiting for your response.

Apparently, seven months after the exchange with E, she decided to stir up some drama in the family. On my birthday.

Oct 24 2019 | From E
Hi Grandson, I think of you daily & wish I could
give you a birthday hug. Wondering if there is
a great grand baby on the way? I want to wish
you a wonderful birthday & all the happiness
you deserve! Love, grandma

To E
Thank you for the birthday wishes. There is no
baby on the way yet.

Then M messaged me from a new account. At first, I didn't see the messages.

From M
I hope this message finds you well. I just got a message from my mom... your bio Grandma E... and she remarked that you tried to reach me via phone 2.5 years ago and that I didn't want anything to do with you... is this true or is she getting fake news?
Because I do want a relationship and only spoke to you via Facebook and you did not want a relationship and I respected that. I pray my mom did not say something to you that made you skittish... there is more to that story for another day.

Oct 27 2019 | From M
I do not believe I deserve no reply... but this will be my last attempt to connect out of respect for you.

Nov 8, 2019 | From M
I don't know if you have been getting my messages, but please reach out to me. We don't have to have a relationship if you don't want, but I would like to clear a few things up.

To M
Hi M, apologies for missing your messages. I just got your email. Is this a new account you are sending from? Apparently it was automatically marked as spam. It sounds like E is

confused. I never told her that you were being
rude or ignoring me or anything like that.

From M
Did you ever talk to her about anything else...
like your childhood? Or is this your only
communication?

What was this line of questioning? I did not understand what I had been roped into.

To M
She sent me several messages about Polio and
her late husband. She also sent me birthday
wishes and I thanked her. She asked me if there
were babies on the way and I told her not yet.
I wasn't really pursuing a conversation but she
seemed like a nice and very old lady so I didn't
want to let her down. We didn't say anything
about my childhood or anything personal like
that.

Then M, feeling the need to defend himself, decided to loop me in on family drama
between his wife and his mother.

From M
At the risk of making you not want anything
to do with this side of your family, I am
going to send you her latest message to me.
Now understand, she doesn't have anything to
say to any of her sons and when she does, it
is fantastic stuff she says.

Now, before you read this... I never walked away from you and I wasn't there at your birth... your mother told me she was pregnant and didn't want me to be a part of it. I was young and selfish and was ok with that. I never knew if she actually had a child and whether it was a boy or girl. By the time I grew up and started caring, I had forgotten her name and even the state where it all happened. Sorry I don't know you and missed out on your life. Here is the letter that my mom sent my wife.

Forwarded From E:
I went back & looked at Alex's message to me & it said, "I spoke w M 2 years ago"—that would make it a total of 3 years ago now. I didn't know about his contact till 2 years after the fact. I had no bearing on his attitude w M! It seems like I get blamed for everything. I learned about Alex from someone's DNA test & he showed up! I don't think you realize that I knew of Alex 29.5 years ago. M went to see Alex when he was born & walked away, not assuming any responsibility. M told me about Alex 29.5 years ago—& Alex had to live a life of abuse he told me. M is acting like he just found out about him. I have told his brothers, over the years, that M had a son out there & I had a 1st born grand baby somewhere. I had no idea that I would ever find him!

I started to get frustrated at this. I did not want to be a part of this drama, and it seemed incredibly immature for these adults – strangers – to involve me in it.

To M
I see. I think I know what she is referencing.
She kept sending me info about different members of her family, so I asked "what can you
tell me about M?" She ignored the question,
but when I asked a second time she said she
wouldn't discuss you. In my reply I mentioned
that my stepfather was not a good man, but I
never said I "lived a life of abuse". I'm sorry
to hear that there is family drama!

From M
Yes... sorry about that... but actually I speak
to my family and have a good relationship...
she is the one who has ostracised her entire
family. At the time you were talking to her, I
was probably the one she was mad at. Currently
she isn't talking to any of us.

The animosity between M and his mother was uninteresting to me. I wanted to
extricate myself from it, but felt like I was supposed to reassure him that I didn't share
her distasteful view of him.

To M
I don't have any resentment or ill will towards
you for being young and foolish. I promise
you that. And I definitely know that my mom
didn't maintain connection with you. I'm not
upset with you or anyone. It's all just part
of my story. I am not totally against having a
relationship, but I just don't know what that
looks like. We are strangers, so I don't know

how to speak or what to speak about. I am glad
that the communication line is open though.

From M
Going forward I would like to have at least an
email relationship with you and only talk about
pleasant things... LOL.

To M
that works for me

From M
So glad... from what I see, you are a bright
man with a beautiful wife... you build your own
computers? Wow

To M
I have done so as a hobby sometimes. Where did
you see that? I never know what info is out
there about me

From M
Your resume on your website

To M
Oh okay

From M
I will send an email and let you know about my
life and you can respond if you wish when you
wish.

To M
sounds good

M's mother messaged me the next day, seemingly still intent on drawing sides. What followed was a confusing chain of forwarded emails.

Nov 9 2019 | From E
Alex, maybe you should read the entire email
that M sent to our whole family. I'm forwarding
it here.

Forwarded From M:
Hello, Family.
I struggled on who to include on this email, but
ultimately I decided the family needs to know
what Mom is doing with her gossip and twisted
view of facts. I believe you, Mom, have warped
many things in the past with your perceptions.
Here is the message you just sent to my wife via
FB messenger… broken up so that I can respond
to each section.

MOM: "I went back & looked @ Alex's message to

me & it said, "I spoke w M 2 years ago"—that would make it a total of 3 years ago now.

RESPONSE: So, either Alex is a liar or something is wrong with Mom. The first time I had ever heard that Alex even existed was 2 years ago… from now… when I received a Facebook message from him that read, "you don't know me but I believe I am your son". He found me via R and Q I believe while searching for "medical history" as he told me on his Facebook message. The history of my relationship with Alex started there.

MOM: "I didn't know about his contact till 2 years after the fact. I had no bearing on his attitude w M! It seems like I get blamed for everything. I learned about Alex from someone's DNA test & he showed up! I don't think you realize that I knew of Alex when his Mother was 3 months pregnant."

RESPONSE: How? And why haven't you said any-thing about this over the years? Either you did not know or you did not respect anybody… me… enough to tell or talk to me about this.

MOM: "M went to see Alex when he was born & walked away, not assuming any responsibility."

RESPONSE: This is not true… either formulated by your own mind, or you got some serious misinformation. The only thing I ever knew about the possibility of having a child was when I received a letter from the state he is from that I was soon to be the father of an unborn child. I contacted the mother and she stated she was pregnant and did not want me to be a part of it. I was about 23 and traveling and I was OK with that. That was the last I ever heard. Over the years and more recently I wondered if she had the child and if she did, whether it was a boy or girl. But that is as far as it went because I had since forgotten her name or even the state where the one-night stand happened.

MOM: "M told me about Alex 29.5 years ago—& Alex had to live a life of abuse he told me. M is acting like he just found out about him. I have told his brothers, over the years, that M had a son out there & I had a 1st born grand baby somewhere. I had no idea that I would ever find him!"

RESPONSE: I ask my brothers… is this true? She told you that I had a son and you guys never told me about this? Now I know Mom is lying because I never told anybody about "Alex" 29.5 years ago. I barely talked to Mom and Dad during this time period when I was a traveling salesman and didn't know about Alex… only that I could possibly be a father over the years.

MOM: "I raised Q & M & never walked away. You probably won't believe me but I had to put the truth out there. M has always known about Alex but never tried to give him love & support—much less find him."

RESPONSE: And you wonder why I don't believe anything you say. You make serious claims about your step-father and expect to be believed and here you are with such a confabulated story that is not true in any way.

I don't know where to go from here. Sorry that my brothers have to get this email. Regretfully, M

PS… Alex has never spoken to me, we only had 2 FB messages and he has yet to respond to a message I sent him a few weeks ago after Mom made these fantastic claims.

From E
M did tell me that he had a son 29 yrs ago. It was M's wife, not me that said M was so excited about hearing from you & thought it might be my words about him that made you not as receptive! I wish you hadn't told M what I said to you. He has never told the truth in his life. I feel betrayed by you. A sweet old lady.

These messages were jarring, signed off with an accusation towards me of betrayal. I was stunned, but didn't reply.

M sent me an incredibly lengthy email with his life story. He wrote about his mom remarrying, and his adoptive dad. He was always in trouble as a kid, pulling pranks and being mischievous. He joined the army, went to college, and claimed to have smoked a joint with a famous movie star. He got kicked out of college for his failing grades, and got kicked out of the army for getting into fist fights with officers. He funneled his hatred of his mother and himself into years of degeneracy and partying, wherein he had the encounter with my mother. He got married, divorced, went back to school, got married again, cheated on his second wife, and got divorced again. He became a born-again Christian, met his third wife, and started a new career. They adopted three children.

I replied with a brief life story of my own – a proto-memoir in email form. I wrote about how I was adopted by my stepfather, who forced my mother to stay home in spite of her advanced degree. I told him about the abuse, and how I resolved to be nothing like my stepfather, and would never touch drugs or alcohol. I told him about my successes and struggles at school, how I developed a love for computers, and how I met my wife. I wrote about how my depression got really bad, my parents' divorce, and coping with PTSD. I told him about school, work, my interests and my passions.

```
From M
Quite a solemn story, I will reply more later
when I have time to digest. Meanwhile, here are
some pics of your extended family.
```

```
Nov 10 2019 | From M
So, I have had time now to read your life
summary a few times and I have to say I am
very impressed with you and your character. You
became a man so much faster than I did and your
impact on your family made me weep. Thanks for
contribution to your world.

I am so sorry I was not around to be your father
and that you had to live parts of the life you
did. Although I am sure that this shaped you
into the man you are today, there are regrets
on my part.

There are things in my life that I wish I could
go back and change... but would I if I had the
```

chance? I don't know... because they too made me who I am and led me to my wife and wonderful children. If I could combine things I would, but this is all fantasy.

I am a believer in perspective and I know that you have a different perspective than I do on certain things, such as social media, relationships and the idea of us being strangers. I respect your perspective but also want to relay that I have a different one. We only live once and relationships are the single most important thing that God gives us in this life that allow us to share Him and ourselves with others. We do not know how long each of us has left on this planet and we must take advantage of each moment. I wish you did not feel the way you do regarding social media so that we could share what we have with each other over the long distances until we meet. Not that we should comment and post and act like we know each other so well, but to share pictures and moments of our lives that we have mostly missed out on. But again, I recognize and respect your perspective on this and it is not mine to change... but I wanted to share my thoughts.

I pray that we don't go to long without connecting more than we are and that we can become more than just DNA.

Again, I am proud that some of my DNA made such a great man.

This message left a bad taste. I didn't care to hear about how he is, in effect, grateful that he abandoned me because it led him to his current family. I was never asking him to profess a choice between the two, so the fact that he felt the need to make the point seemed immature.

M's mother emailed again, this time sending a nearly incomprehensible set of forwarded text messages from various members of their family.

Nov 12 2019 | From E
This was a copied text sent by Q to me on the 17th of March, 2018.

Q told me he found out by R through a DNA test. I never talked to R about it. Note the part where I say that I already knew & his age of around 27yrs. Alex was 28. It seems Q has the same problem remembering that M does. They are cut from the same cloth! Don't quote the Bible to me & don't say that I push people away. You 2 do the pushing. There isn't a matter of forgiveness here, there is a matter of sociopathic sons that are abusive to their Mother. Always backing up to start over. No, I didn't tell Alex the real medical problem but I am now. The Bible says to stay away from these people! Q , you defiled my Dad's website by putting my pedi file stepfather next to my pic. That was deliberate as there is no reason for him to be there. You know my Dad was of great character & he would be furious. The sad part about this is that I've lost my grandkids. They were always your weapons tho, Q. Mom's Mind still works. I don't want any reply's from anyone. I don't want to hear from either of you again. I'm the only one that takes

constant abuse & those days are over.
Your vicious, gossiping Mother

She continued to send even more unattributed and indecipherable forwarded messages, attempting to reveal to me some 'truth' about their family.

From E
Begin forwarded message:
M's son Alexander. I see a replica! My grandson!
He lives in Atlanta. He's 26 or 27. So you were
right.
M has made up for it with the 3 he's adopted.
That doesn't speak for Alex. I never knew him &
he was abandoned by M. M knew she was pregnant
& saw her after delivery & disappeared. I had
a mean stepfather, so I can imagine what Alex
might have endured. M tells me what a lousy
mother I am constantly but I never gave him up
even tho I had no means of support. I never
knew this child!
Why have you never mentioned this for 26 years?
Just curious.
So now, I'm to blame?
Huh? Where the heck do you get that from?
Like it was up to me to shed light on it, not
M?
Just curious why you've not said anything for
26 years. How does that make you to blame? You
were shedding light on it today… Again, just
curious.
I had it buried in back of my brain. It was
when told me that I had lousy parenting skills
that I started to recollect that my stepfather
tried to get me to put you two in an orphanage.

He wouldn't let my mother baby sit for you any more. I fought to keep you kids & M turned his back on his own flesh & blood, never worrying about what he might be enduring. I started recalling everything M had done that was not loving & I remembered that. Remember that M said that he wanted to be estranged from me. Well, he estranged his own child too. & he never had a face until today & I didn't know you could ever find him—didn't know about DNA finding him. I just accepted it. But, M knew!

I struggled to comprehend any of this. I really wanted to fully check out from the drama. M messaged me, apologizing for the mess.

```
From M
Once again... sorry Alex... I won't be sur-
prised if I don't hear from you again.
```

```
To M
It's unfortunate, but I'm not going to concern
myself with it!
```

```
Nov 23 2019 | From M
Just so you know... even if we don't communi-
cate, you are in my thoughts and prayers.
```

```
Nov 25 2019 | To M
Thanks, I hope you guys have a good thanksgiving
and merry Christmas.
```

```
From M
You too. Do you mind sending your address so
we can send you a card?
```

I winced, but after the family drama I had been exposed to, I was afraid of what would happen if I rejected this request.

```
To M
Sure. But please don't share it with anyone
else.
```

```
Dec 25, 2019 | From M
Merry Christmas
```

22

I DID NOT ABANDON YOU

Over the next year, M sent sporadic messages with various life updates. I tried to be polite and receptive, not knowing where things would go or what he really wanted from the relationship.

Mar 6 2020 | From M
Hope all is well with you and your family. Just thinking of you today and how your days are going. We are planning a family road trip. We plan to stay in our RV and have fireworks wars with the other cabins on the river... should be fun. Hope you have some fun plans coming out of the winter into the spring and then the summer. Just wanted to drop you a line and let you know I am still alive and open to any conversation.

To M
Thanks for checking in. That sounds like a fun trip - we do a similar thing on 4th of july. No big plans here, just staying busy with work, and putting in some job applications to see what's out there. Otherwise just doing some house projects and saving money.

Apr 9 2020 | From M
Just wanted to keep you in the loop. Grandma E
fell a few weeks ago and fractured her shoulder.
During xrays they found a brain tumor. They
operated on it and got most of it. Now she is
on chemo and radiation and with the COVID 19
circulating... things are dicey. All of this
per report from C as she still has chosen not
to see me or my brother, Q.

To M
So sorry to hear! I will certainly keep you all
in my prayers. I hope you are staying safe and
healthy otherwise.

Jun 26 2020 | From M
Just had a family reunion. Here's a picture.

Jul 1 2020 | From M
Did you receive my last email with the pic?

To M
Sorry for not replying - it's been really busy
over here. I did get the picture. Thanks for
sharing that with me.

Oct 27 2020 | From M
I believe your Grandmother is leaving us
tonight. She is comfortable.

To M
So sorry to hear. I'm glad she's comfortable.
My best wishes to you and your whole family.

After this, I only heard from M twice over the next two years.

Dec 25 2020 | From M
I hope you are having a great Christmas during
this tumultuous year. I pray you and yours are
safe and stay healthy.

Aug 15 2021
M would like to follow you on Instagram.

Aug 19 2021 | From M
Alex... no need to reply. Just wanted to say I
am thinking of you and praying for you. Hope
your marriage and life is going well through
Covid. Stay safe and God bless you and yours.

Oct 19 2021
M would like to follow you on Instagram.

Oct 20 2021 | From M
I hope you have a great upcoming birthday!!

Aug 1 2022
M would like to follow you on Instagram.

Then, M decided to express some frustrations.

Sep 9 2022 | From M
Alex.. I've tried enough to be just a bit in
your life... but you block me at every turn.
That has been hurtful and maybe that's just who
you are or who I am and I need to respect that.
Maybe I don't deserve any type of relationship
with you, but life's too short to squander these
types of relationships. You only live once so I
pray you don't miss out on things that could be
more important than you think. You don't need
to respond... just wanted you to know. May God
bless you in this life and may we meet again
in eternity. I will let you go and not bother
you any longer... son.

This felt unfairly accusatory.

To M
Hi M, perhaps I missed something. I see 2 emails
from you in 2021. One was a simple birthday
message, and the other said "no need to reply".
This is the first message I've gotten from you
in 2022. Maybe you tried to connect another way

and it got lost? I definitely have not blocked
you in any way. I certainly don't want to be
hurtful. Can you let me know what I might've
missed?

From M
I feel it's pretty clear that you don't desire
any communication from me which is evidenced
by really no communication from you... I can
respect that but don't understand it. The
latest was you appeared in my Instagram feed
and I followed you and then you disappeared.
I don't want to be a child and push this any
further... just wanted to let you know I wanted
to at least know you a bit from afar... but it
feels in vain.

I didn't appreciate his victimized approach.

Sep 10 2022 | To M
I see - the instagram thing certainly wasn't
personal, and I did not know you were affected.
Please don't misunderstand.

I'll be very honest with you (and I hope you
don't mind this lengthy email): 2021 and 2022
have been some of the hardest years of my life.
In 2021 I left my career to run a fundraiser
that I really believed in. I inadvertently
ended up in a leadership position, and I went to
work raising money for charity. Well, it turned
out that the "friend" and previous founder took

advantage of me and stole millions from the charity on his way out the door. That turned into me, as the face of the company, getting hundreds of death threats for the past year.

So, I had to set my instagram to private and effectively remove all of my followers because they were posting my address and sending threats to my family. I apologize if you felt like that sent a rude message - if you send a follow request I will accept it, but be warned that I very rarely use any social media these days.

My wife and I have been trying to start our family for years with difficulty, and I'm happy to share with you that Natalie got pregnant early this year, and we're expecting our first child. But this year has brought a whole new set of trials. Her pregnancy has been high-risk and she has been in the hospital repeatedly to stop premature labor. She then got fired from her job for being in the hospital, and I had to shut down my charity fundraiser. We also had a serious suicide attempt in the family.

It has been a terribly stressful two years, and our focus has just been on taking care of the people closest to us. You have sent me a few emails, and they were appreciated, but I just truly didn't know where to begin replying. And, I hadn't heard from you in 11 months now, so I assumed it wasn't something you were looking for. In the nightmare of the past couple years, figuring out how to properly engage with you seemed impossible. I hope you can understand that connecting with my biological father is a very daunting task that requires more care and attention than I have had available. I'm trying to shake off the weight of the past couple years and get my mindset right to start my own journey of fatherhood in just a couple months, which is absolutely my priority. I didn't know you were getting hurt by that. I was not trying to shut the door on you.

Sorry for the dump of negativity! Just trying to share what I've been up against, and to let you know that I haven't meant anything personally against you.

From M
I appreciate this letter. I am truly sorry for the hardships you are facing right now and have faced. Thanks for clearing the air for the communication bit. Perception is always key. When I emailed you those few times... with the expectation that you did not have to reply... yes... a reply would have been great. Insofar as to let me know that you were interested in just a little communication back and forth. When that did not occur, nor did I ever hear from you over the past couple of years... I fell back on your original sentiment that you did not want to pursue a relationship with me... I understood, but have always held out hope that this would change... it did not seem to. I'm not

looking for an all-encompassing relationship but since life is what it is... and short... I don't want to miss out on something with you if I can help it. You don't owe me anything but this is not about owing another but having something that some fathers and sons only dream about.

I hope you realize that I truly did think about whether you were a girl or a boy over the years and whether you were doing well.

My life is great now that I have hindsight on what it means to be a man. My faith and family relationships are great. Mom and Dad are both deceased and the relationship with Mom left a bitter taste, but I forgive her and pray that she is in heaven with Dad. My relationship with your uncle C is great but the relationship with uncle Q is lacking as he doesn't have much to do with C or me over the past few decades. I did talk to him a few days ago and he seems to be doing fine. My other 2 brothers (twins) who I have never met outside of Facebook are doing great and we are planning a get together over the next few years. I really hope it happens. K just got married and both are living in Montana. My 2 boys are a handful and I am still learning how to parent them. They come from a troubled childhood and seem to have some genetic disposition carried on from their bio-parents that we can't decipher. My daughter is a joy and is excelling in school. She asks about you when she sees your picture in my office. "Someday" I tell her.

Well those are my thoughts and I hope we can
at least stay in touch through Instagram with
pictures (if you think its safe) or Facebook...
or even email. Would love to watch your life
from afar if that is all there will be. That
will be enough for now.

That felt like more blaming. Things spiraled from there.

To M
Thanks for your note. Perception is certainly
key, and it's perhaps a reminder that you
shouldn't take something personally when you
don't know what someone is going through.

I want to be clear about something.

I understand that you have a desire to get to
know me. I also understand that mistakes of your
past deserve forgiveness, and I have forgiven
them. I also understand that it was ages ago,
and you are a different person now.

But please try to understand things from my
perspective here. The reality is that as of
right now, we do not know each other. All I
do know, is that a stranger abandoned me when
I was born. That same person turned up in my
inbox after 11 months of no contact to accuse
ME of abandoning HIM.

I hope you can see how that is inappropriate

and hurtful. Regardless of how things have changed, you are the person that walked away from me. You are the person that had the most transformative effect on my life out of anyone. It fundamentally defined how I grew up and who I became, for better or worse - it left a mark. All the ignored emails in the world wouldn't make you the victim here, and I do not think it's right for you to paint me as someone who is rejecting you. So, to tell me that YOU feel abandoned or rejected, is very hurtful. The reality is you abandoned me. In fact, I was the one that found you and reached out.

I'm trying to be very clear here. I understand that you want more communication with me, but the only foundation we have is that you abandoned me at birth. Emailing me out of the blue to tell me that I am being hurtful to you and rejecting you is an attitude of self-centeredness - and it does not fill me with any confidence that I can put my trust in you. You could have easily and simply sent me an email telling me what kind of relationship you are hoping for, instead of blaming ME for our distance.

I don't want you to refer to us as "father and son". And yes, you are correct that I said years ago I do not want a relationship. In your sporadic messages you've said "no need to reply" plenty of times, but clearly you did not actually mean that, and I didn't know you had higher expectations. I've just gotten sparse emails, and haven't known how to respond. I don't know what your intentions are, or whether you are a person with integrity as you claim to be. At this point you are a stranger. If you let me know clearly what kind of relationship you want, I will let you know what I would be comfortable with. I'm not shutting the door. I'm just letting you know that making progress in our communication cannot begin with you painting me as the party to blame for our distance. I hope you can see that I've tried to give you as much grace here as I can. I could have easily seen your email where you accused me out of the blue of being hurtful, and moved on - because I do not deserve that. It's not my responsibility to do the emotional labor to try to have a respectful dialogue after the disrespectful email you sent me, but I am doing that.

I hope you can read this email with some compassion, and see it from where I am sitting. I don't deserve the person who left me at birth to also show up in my inbox making accusations about how I'm hurtful and squandering opportunities. I don't say this with any malice or ill will, just a desire to let you know that I know I deserve more respect than that.

However, you can be clear and let me know what you want, and we can find a place to start.

Sep 11 2022 | From M
I received your last email. Thanks for sharing
your feelings on the subject of fatherhood and
integrity.

My father left me and my older brother when I
was just born and he was about 1 year old.
He left my Mom never to be heard from again
although the grandparents stayed in touch a
few times over the years. Although I never felt
abandoned because my adoptive father was in my
life before I knew it and I grew up with a great
Dad. But the truth is... I was abandoned by a
man who knew me and was already in my life.
Later on in life when I reached adulthood I
reached out to him so that I could get to know
who my biological father was... not for genetic
reasons... but because the relationship with my
blood father was important to me... there is
so much of me in him. Sadly, he wanted nothing
to do with me and only spoke to me once on
the phone for a brief minute and I could never
reach him again. This hurt. i had never done
anything to him but I was willing to ignore
the past and the stories my Mom told to see
if there was anything there for us. He truly
abandoned me.

I tell this story because I DID NOT ABANDON YOU.
You repeated that I had over and over again
in your previous email and maybe you heard
something that never happened or you use that
phrase loosely. Your mom made it clear that she
was raising you alone and did not want me to

participate. I received a letter saying I was the father of an unborn child and that the mom wished to reach out to me. When I made the call, she stated she was pregnant and she was going it alone. I honestly did not remember who she was as it was a couple of months after the fact and I was very active with "relationships". And I remember there not being much time to ask questions as she made it clear she was letting me know out of respect and then she was gone. I never met you... I didn't even know if she followed through and if you were a girl or a boy. Over the years I racked my brain and the internet to see if there was a way to find you but alas that was not possible. I DID NOT ABANDON YOU... I was not let in your life and life went on.

I previously said that perception is everything and I think you took that as something I should take into account. Because I brought it up, I did take that into account. I know my perception but I appreciate you thinking that maybe I was wrong. I don't believe I was. I take people at their word and their actions speak louder than words. My perception was that you made it clear that you did not want a significant relationship when we started and I could not tell if you would be open to something later on... only that you found me because of health information... not because you had any interest in knowing your biological sperm donor (I didn't use father). I still held out hope and sent a few emails with a few updates and happy wishes... with the occasional short but limited response from you and then no response to the last one or two. "No need to reply" doesn't mean "don't reply".;; It means "I don't want to seem like I am pressuring you to respond but I would love to continue to hear about your life." Maybe I should have made that clearer. I stopped writing for a while because not only did I respect you and your space and your decision to only want genetic information... but also because you did not seem to be interested in pursuing a relationship with me. Little did I know of your circumstances and I am sorry that NOT knowing caused me to doubt your interest.

Now if everything I said just now leads you to doubt my integrity, I am sorry. But your accusation that I accused you of abandoning me is not true. I accused you of making me believe you did not want to pursue anything deeper or more important. Abandonment infers being there in the first place... you never were so I don't feel abandoned.

You stated, "I don't deserve the person who left me at birth to also show up in my inbox making accusations about how I'm hurtful and squandering opportunities."

I DID NOT ABANDON YOU... please understand that. I did not "show up in your inbox" you reached out to me and gave me great joy that you existed with hope that this was a beginning. I also don't believe my initial email about being

hurt should have been taken as accusatory. I
even attempted to make it clear that maybe it
was you and maybe it was me and that I need
to respect that. If my attempt at telling you
that I am hurt by the lack of response causes
you to be that defensive... you certainly do
have some resentment toward me that would need
to be resolved before moving on.

I am a man who had a son that he did not
know... was not there for his birth... hoped
his entire life that this child was doing well
and that someday I would know him or her. I
ask for forgiveness for the actions that led
to your birth... the sex before marriage...
and that this action caused you to live a life
without knowing me or me knowing you. But I
don't ask for forgiveness for abandoning you
because I never did that, nor was it my choice
to not be there. I do know that my actions as
a non-believer back in those days led to a lot
of consequences and I have been forgiven by God
for those.

He was trying to rewrite history, and even contradicted his earliest words to me, in
those first messages. His message was only about himself, and how his pains absolved his
actions. I'd seen that before. I was done with this.

To M
I was hoping to see accountability and humility
in your reply, and I didn't, which saddens me.

I did not send you my long message to bring the
past into debate, but merely to clearly illus-

trate why your attitude in your messages was inappropriate. Yet, you seem only interested in defending your actions in the past. I was quite surprised to see you so adamantly claim you didn't abandon your child. In fact, I have paper transcriptions from 1990 recorded by my mother of your conversation. A conversation in which she asked you for child support, asked you to appear in court with her, and asked you for your contact information so she could stay in touch. Perhaps time has formed a different memory for you, but it's all there in the transcript. In the call, you agreed to the child support and said "let me see my baby." She replied "I will let you see your baby." After that she never heard from you again, and never received the child support.

I am not interested in raking you over the coals for making the mistakes of a foolish young man. I'm also not interested in he-said-she-said of the past. It's okay to be human and I hold no resentment for any of that. It's just disappointing and strange that you would rather take time now to tell me that you were somehow a victim of those proceedings, instead of just owning up to the fact that your actions left a child fatherless. The fact remains that the younger you DID have the capacity and ability to establish a presence in my life, and if you wanted to do it there is nothing that could have stopped you. Perhaps my mother made no demands, but she did not hide her phone number or contact information from you.

I do not doubt that after a time you had a change of heart and looked for me, and could not find me. That is understandable and I empathize with that. But in that moment where she called you, you DID have a choice. To posture now as if you did NOT have a choice lacks any sense of accountability.

Instead of reaching out again with open arms and warmth, you told me about how YOUR feelings were hurt.

I was quite open and vulnerable with you about my family and life in my previous email, and instead of asking any questions or showing any interest, you told me about how difficult this is for YOU.

I told you that I felt I deserved better than to have your feelings thrust upon me as if you are entitled to my attention. Instead of any humility, you told me about how YOU were abandoned.

I asked you to explain in clear terms what kind of relationship you want, and you instead went to defend yourself at length.

It seems clear now that you believe that you are offering me an opportunity and a privilege to connect with a biological father. An opportunity you never had. And it seems clear that you think I would be foolish to squander

this privilege you were never afforded. But
that is just another example of this dynamic
having to be about you.

My strong advice to you is seek a counselor or
therapist. Perhaps if you share these messages
with that therapist they can help you see how
you have lacked the humility and accountability
that this situation needs. How you have made
this situation about you, and your feelings,
instead of about the person on the other end.
How you are so wounded from the rejection
by your own father, that you are placing
entitlement and rude expectations upon me so
you can gain closure on your own pain.

However, I do not have the time or space for
the stress that you are bringing me here.
I empathize with the fact that you want the
satisfaction of connecting with a "lost son"
but you currently lack the ability to do so
in a way that isn't solely about yourself and
your own pride, and sense of what is just,
important, or expected.

I will do the last bit of labor for you, and
write this out. The words you could have said
at any point were:

"Alex, when I was a foolish young man, I made
the choice to not retain any contact information for your mother, nor provide support, nor
be in your life. When I regretted that later,
it was too late to find you. For that I am

sorry, as my own actions left you fatherless. This is something that especially pains me, as I too missed out on a childhood with my bio-dad. Though I can't change the past, I would love to have a chat one day if you ever find time for it. If you will allow it, I would like to learn about you and what I've missed."

Instead of doing any of that, you sent me messages about your family and children as if they were already my family, you denied your own accountability, you told me about how you were hurt by our distance, and about how I would be squandering an opportunity if I didn't reply, were passive-aggressive in your messages of "no need to reply" which apparently meant the opposite, and foisted your sense of abandonment from your own father onto me as if it somehow outweighs or invalidates my experience.

I truly wish you all the best. I tried to open the door, and I tried to see what could be beneficial about pursuing deeper conversation. But I just don't have the ability at this juncture to make room for reconnecting with a bio-father who insists on his own pride. Right now this is stress and a burden that I neither want nor deserve. Perhaps you can reflect on it, and one day you will look back and understand.

From M
Sorry... that is not at all how the conversation went. But I must say... not how I remember it. I

admit I could be wrong and if I am I apologize.
It was so long ago. All I remember is wondering
about you and going through times of looking
on ancestry and such to see if there were any
connections or there looking for me.

I am not wanting to engage in back and forth
accusatory emails. This is not going to be a
healthy relationship and it appears you have a
ways to go with your opinion of me and I am not
wanting to engage in this type of condescending
conversion any longer. Maybe I will read this
entire email someday but for now I could not
get past the 2nd paragraph. Blessings on your
problems and call me if you wish to engage in a
more adult and productive conversation and/or
relationship.

Sep 12 2022 | From M
I finally read the entire thing... and like I
said, it is all about perception. I understand
and value your perception but wanted to answer
your statements/feelings so that you would
better understand mine.,.. I don't think you
do.

It is hard to be humble when unfounded accusations are slung my way.

While I admit that the conversation may have
occurred the way the transcript recorded it, I
truly do not remember that conversation. Only
that I received a letter from some agency that

stated I was the father of an unborn child and
I could respond. I remember responding with the
claim that she was raising the child by herself
and only felt compelled to let me know. So I
apologize if I neglected my responsibility...
that is not me now.

Now, regarding me sharing my feelings. No
matter our pasts... I too have the right to have
feelings and to feel hurt. You don't own that.
And expressing those feelings is how people
relate. To not respect others' feelings is how
we are unable to communicate. I reached out
to you with how I felt everything was going
between us and the first two emails that you
returned were cordial and I learned what was
going on with you.

Regarding me making it about how difficult it
is for me: This is simply not true. With the
limited information I have of you and your
family... one lengthy email... I offered what
I thought was appropriate. My wife and I prayed
that night for you and your wife as well in
regards to finances and child bearing. I did
not feel comfortable asking any more questions
about this personal stuff because i still felt
that you were trying to distance yourself from
a relationship with me.

You say you feel you deserve better than to have
my feeling thrust upon you? Did you really say
this? You do not deserve any better than this.
Expressing feelings is how humans communicate.

To say you deserved better is prideful... that which you cast upon me. If you truly believe you deserve better than to have me express my feelings to you, we are not alike. I don't deserve you as a son... this I know. I don't deserve my wife, my children, and my salvation. My sins are many and when I get what I don't deserve that is a real good thing... and when I don't get what I do deserve that is a real good thing as well.

I've made it clear what I desire from this relationship. I don't believe I am 'offering' you anything. I believe God is sovereign and in control and He offers. I do see an opportunity that I BELIEVE should not be squandered, and I would be remiss if I dismissed that and said nothing.

I have closure with my father's abandonment... and if he were still alive and decided to reach out for a better relationship... I would. I am not one to hold grudges and understand that life hits you hard and you make mistakes. I also understand my Mom and how she would drive people away in her life. It is quite demeaning to say something like this to another and I hope you know that. I don't need a counselor or therapist. I have a loving wife and other brothers in Christ who I can go to for advice, admonishment and rebuke. My wife is a teacher and counselor and I bounce things off of her, I see that your advice is "strong" advice and i appreciate that, but I hope you

can go back and read your responses to my
simple 1st email as over the top... as if you
still resent me for my sins of the past...
because in no way did any of my previous emails
deserve your condemnation... maybe a little
more communication and clarification... which
is how it started with your first 2 emails...
and then you went off the rails.

My wanting to connect with you IS about me. I
want it. I desire it. I can't make it about
you... you have to do that. I would love for you
to want it, but it is in no way pride. My pride
would have me walk away already but my wife
told me I have to explain my feelings better.
Even if you don't want it about my feelings...
it's all I have to offer right now.

Regarding your script you offered me: I didn't
say this because I did not believe it to be
true. However if this is truly what happened,
that is my desire. How awful it was to read
a transcript like that... I am sure. Sorry
that I abandoned you and did not grow up
until way later. I would like a father/son
relationship... if that is still possible. But
I am who I am and I express myself and my
feelings.

You don't know the meaning of passive aggressive. "No need to reply" was to take pressure
off of you if you had no desire to reply, which
I believed you may not have had. Maybe I was
wrong, but this was not "passive aggressive".

```
Pressure and stress come with establishing
a relationship like this. It has been very
stressful for me as well, but I welcome it if
it means connecting with you. I forgive you for
all this.

Love, M
```

I only knew him through these messages, and getting to this point was an excruciating, slow-motion train wreck. Five years of surreal, obtuse emails laced with breath-holding malaise. I did not have it in me to pursue a relationship with yet another person who could not see past themselves. Someone who had not done the deep work of getting better.

I went no-contact with a father for the second time in my life.

23

EARLY ARRIVAL

Natalie and I started trying to have a child in 2020. Due to complications with her cycle and a new diagnosis of Polycystic Ovary Syndrome, getting pregnant via classic methods proved fruitless. By Summer of 2020, we sought medical help.

Natalie has a lifelong phobia of needles. When needing to get a shot or vaccine, she has often requested that I be present to distract her, pin down an autonomously flailing limb, or hug her tightly. So, it was a great shock to both of us when the doctors determined that a new cocktail of hormones and drugs to counteract the PCOS would need to be injected in Natalie daily at home.

She was brave, and already filled with love for a child that didn't even exist yet. She resolved to go through with it. Twice a day I injected her with the medicines as she shook and wept, and I tried to tell jokes to distract her. We hoped that these methods would permit her menstrual cycle to work as expected, and each month we went to the clinic to see if it had resulted in a successful pregnancy. And each month we got bad news. Too many follicles, too few follicles, lining too thick, lining too thin, ovulation interrupted, hormone levels too low, hormone levels too high... Each month the doctor adjusted the cocktail of medicines, and each month we tried again, hoping the new combination of injected hormones would unlock her body's ability to ovulate on cue. She had a few instances of promising signs, followed by intense pain and the passing of heavy blood clots – potentially early miscarriages.

After a year of this, we both accepted that we'd likely never be biological parents. She started to hate herself, blaming herself for a biological glitch she couldn't control. She knew how much being a father meant to me, and she felt she was taking it away from me. I told her repeatedly that I wanted nothing more than to just be with her. I told her that if parenthood wasn't going to happen, we would be okay. It was hard for her to believe me.

"I feel like I'm trying to do something that's just impossible," she said. "Like a whale trying to fly to the moon."

Then in February of 2022, we got good news. It worked, and Natalie was pregnant. Natalie was relieved that she was able to finally coerce her body into cooperating with our plans, and we started getting excited about the future. Then the rest of our lives imploded.

First, the house. Our heater broke, and the technicians were puzzled as to what happened. Our dishwasher broke down, soaking our dishes in grimy backed up water. Our freezer burst internally, leaking water everywhere. And then the water main line from the street to the house exploded underground, flooding our front yard and costing us thousands in our water bill.

As we worked on the expensive tasks of replacing our heater, dishwasher, refrigerator, and digging up our front yard to replace the main water pipe, Natalie got a call from her parents. Her mother set plans to donate a kidney to a stranger, her parents announced their official separation, and there was a serious suicide attempt in Natalie's family.

Natalie's pregnancy symptoms hit her hard. She vomited so forcefully she broke every blood vessel in both eyes, and for several weeks the whites of her eyes were a terrifying blood-red. Still, she powered through, and kept working. She checked in with her boss routinely, and would stay up very late finishing her tasks to compensate for lost mornings of vomiting and dizziness.

Then, just days after her boss congratulated her for performing well, her job fired her. They confirmed multiple times she was not only meeting expectations, they commended her in staff ceremonies for exceeding them. They did not want to pay for her maternity leave. The post-pandemic job market was slim, but it wasn't long before Natalie found work again. She'd soon lose this job to a wave of layoffs.

The baby was unusually low, and kicked. Kicked hard, constantly. On a checkup, a frightening development was discovered: her cervix was found to have dilated early, and we were rushed to the delivery ward at 21 weeks. We stayed overnight, but delivery did not occur. We were sent home with instructions to be cautious, and for Natalie to remain bed-bound for the rest of the pregnancy.

The baby kept kicking at the cervix. Then two weeks later, her mucus plug fell out. We rushed to the delivery ward and stayed overnight once again. A doctor visited us to perform a cervical check on Natalie. She put her hand up... and the doctor SCREAMED. Natalie jolted, gasping in shock.

"Sorry!" the doctor said, yanking her hand back.

"What happened?" Natalie asked.

"He grabbed my hand!"

We laughed in confusion. "What?" Natalie said.

"I have been doing this for thirty years, and I have never had that happen before. He stuck his hand out of your cervix, still inside the amniotic sac, and wrapped his hand around my finger! He was saying hello!"

Natalie was given the option to either stay in the hospital under observation, or to go home and remain on bed rest. We went home. All the while this was happening, I was fracturing my relationship with my biological father, and things with my work were imploding as well. Natalie was depressed and stuck in bed, and I was emotionally frayed beyond capacity. I focused on getting the house ready instead.

On our main level we have three bedrooms and two bathrooms. The primary bedroom is quite small, only distinguished as a primary bedroom by the private bathroom attached. The private bathroom is only really distinguished as a bathroom because of the presence of a toilet and shower – otherwise you wouldn't be blamed for mistaking it for a closet. The other two bedrooms were in use as my office and Natalie's office. We needed to turn one of those into a nursery, while still making room for the potential of us both working from home in the future. So, we needed to finish the basement. Our basement was barren with concrete walls and some pillars that supported the house. Contracting with a family friend, we added an office, a bedroom, and bathroom, and more storage.

The day after the finishing touches were put on the basement, Natalie was diagnosed with preeclampsia and gestational diabetes. The placenta wasn't playing nice with her body, and at another routine checkup they found that her kidneys were near total shutdown. They ordered an emergency induction at 35 weeks.

They administered the induction drug, and her labor began. It was mild at first, and they told us she'd likely be in labor for multiple days. After the first 18 hours, Natalie urged me to go get myself some food. I went out as quickly as I could, got a slice of pizza, and came back. When I entered the room, Natalie looked different. The color had drained from her face.

"I think I peed the bed," she muttered.

"Let me look." I looked under her. It was the most blood I had ever seen in my life. Concealing my panic, I said, "I'm going to go find the nurse."

My pizza went into the trash can, and I raced out and searched the halls for any sign of medical personnel. I found some nurses at the front desk, chatting.

"There is a lot of blood in here. She lost a lot of blood. Can someone come in here quickly?" I asked.

"Sure, someone will come in," they said.

I went back to the room. I did my best to assure Natalie that everything would be okay, and we waited as I distracted Natalie from the lake of blood she was sitting in. No one came.

I went back out, and snapped at them, "Someone needs to come in here! There is a lot of blood. Is the doctor around?"

They shooed me away. A nurse finally came in, and wordlessly started shifting Natalie around to strip the bed of the bloody sheets and throw them away.

"Do we know why she's bleeding? Is the doctor coming?" I interrogated the nurse.

"Okay, y'all just calm down, alright?" she said dismissively.

Moments later the doctor came in. "Looks like the baby is coming sooner than we thought!" she said.

It turned out that the blood was the partial abruption of the placenta. The baby needed to come out quickly, or his oxygen levels could prove fatal. Natalie pushed, screaming. Twenty minutes later, I received our son directly and gave him to Natalie. Peter was born five weeks early in October of 2022, weighing four pounds and 14 ounces.

He thankfully didn't need any time in the NICU. Instead, we stayed at the hospital for three nights, administering a blue light treatment on his jaundiced skin. When we got home, Natalie painted a mural in his nursery – a whale flying to the moon.

24

INTENTIONALITY

I have wanted to be a father for my entire life. Ever since I was young, when other kids would talk about wanting to be an astronaut or a firefighter, I wanted to be a dad. A big part of this was to find some healing. In many ways, I subconsciously felt that I could bring relief to my own inner child by having a child of my own and being the father that I never had. This is a responsibility that would be patently unfair to project onto my child, but I had not unpacked that within myself yet. Instead, parenting was something I studied with academic rigor for two decades. Even in college, I'd often want to have conversations about parenting modalities with friends who would look at me as if I was crazy. They, sensibly, were not thinking about that in that era of their life. Still, I researched and journaled and planned for every definable aspect of child psychology. I am immensely grateful that Natalie cares just as much about the intentionality of child-rearing as I do, and we armed ourselves to be the providers of the most enriching childhood possible.

I will address the rest of this chapter to you, my child. My hope is that you read this when you are grown, and are able to see this as a reflection of the love we have for you, before we even met you. This isn't just about rules and principles, but about sharing the core of who your mother and I are, and the journeys that brought us to you. If you ever wonder why I parented in a certain way, or if you are trying to make sense of your childhood narratives, I hope you'll find insight here. I've known total rejection and absolute belonging. Both experiences shaped me profoundly, and those experiences are the bedrock of how I aim to ensure you are loved and supported.

Perhaps more important than rules for children, is rules for parents. We may not always take you literally, but we aim to always take you seriously. We intend to give you security in an identity we craft for you, and also give you the tools you need to dismantle that identity. We will tell you that you are beautiful, strong, and smart – not as rewards for accomplishing something, but as a natural fact of your existence. We will praise you not for things inherent to your being, but for your choices, your ethic, and your perspective. We will teach you not only how to be safe, but that you *are* safe. We will allow you to struggle against obstacles, so you can gain the hard-won knowledge that obstacles can be overcome. We will grant your four irreducible freedoms in childhood: the freedom to exist in our world, the freedom from having to work to make your environment peaceful and stable, the freedom to experience all emotions, and the freedom to have imaginative and creative play. We will provide structure, discipline, and consequences that aim to encourage self-regulation, rather than conformity. We will put your autonomy and exploration first. Rather than trying to construct you into a particular kind of success, we will create a diverse and rich environment for you to flourish in. We will be clear with our expectations, and differentiate between *values* and *strategies*. We will create family rituals and traditions that affirm you as an invaluable member of our family, and we will be intentional about the norms we set in place. We will be present, we will model healthy conflict, and we will take accountability.

How will we know if we did a good job as parents? Hopefully, as you encounter adulthood and grow into your identity, you are able to claim the following truths and tools for yourself. You choose meaning over expedience, and fulfillment over gratification. You regulate your emotions, accept them without judgment, and express them safely. You embrace embarrassment, and have the resilience to learn from mistakes. You are skeptical of the obvious, question assumptions, and are cautious of simple solutions. You are keenly aware of how your actions impact what's around you, and you understand how your environment influences your choices. You prioritize honesty with empathy, speak with humility, and aim to speak the deep truth. You practice mindfulness, and manage stress actively. You embrace challenge, seek opportunities to grow, and willingly explore the unknown. You understand inequality, seek diversity, and cultivate social responsibility. You have compassion for those who hurt others, and those they hurt. You seek excellence beyond victory, and develop a perspective on success that goes beyond winning. You surround yourself with positive influences and uplift those around you. You recognize manipulation, set healthy boundaries, and communicate openly.

That's our intention. I'm sure it will be messy, haphazard, and full of gut-calls and improvisation. But, we're in this together. And we believe in you.

25

BELIEF

In spite of everything I've experienced over my lifetime, my experiences in the Catholic Church are arguably where I've experienced the most privilege. The Church is an institution filled with flawed people. And those people have caused hurt to so many other people, while the Church gave me a safe space to exist and be loved.

But, my wife and I need to determine how we will raise our children. We see the beauty of the Church, in all of its rites and community. We see the ugliness of the Church, in all of its complicity in abuse of the vulnerable and marginalized. We also see our privilege, as parents who have the resources to take advantage of what the church offers while shielding our children from the slings and arrows. And we see so many people we love fall away from the Church – and we understand why.

So first, we must determine what it is we fundamentally believe, beyond all dogma and catechesis.

We believe that the world is fundamentally good. We believe that matter is the mediator of spirit, not the obstacle or antithesis of it. We believe that the world itself is incarnational. We believe that to be holy is to be whole, to be made whole is to endure ongoing transformation, and to be transformed is to let go. We believe that God is first encountered by seeing God in others, that everything is defined by its connection to everything else, and that salvation is not reached alone. We believe that unity is global, borderless, and transcendent, that the needs of people supersede ideology, and that the same vision can be expressed in many ways. We believe that peace cannot be enforced by war, that justice cannot be produced by competition, and that love cannot be known through exclusion.

We believe that it is our mission to revere the universe as inherently sacramental, let go of everything holding us back from love, be light for those around us, work for justice for the less fortunate, and organize community that points others towards love.

If we build on this from first principles, you could call this way of seeing the world Sacramental Relational Prioritarian Pragmatism. You could call it Panentheistic Non-Dual Mysticism. You could call it being a good person. But, we are content to call it Catholicism.

Building on this further, we can bring in the dogma and catechesis. Humans didn't arise from a man and woman named Adam and Eve. There was no literal great ark with two of every animal. I don't believe that hell exists. Does heaven exist? God, who knows.

What about the Eucharist? I'll put it this way. Maybe someone grows up as a Catholic, and becomes obsessed with the structure and rules. They amass knowledge and wisdom like trinkets stacked in teetering towers and crammed into a hoarder's kitchen, hungrily clinging to a piece of bread as their salvation. They cast shame and derision on anyone who would dare to touch their things without the proper rites, gatekeeping divinity behind incense and ancient scrawlings. Or, maybe their experience with the divinity housed in a single, lowly piece of bread opens them to encountering divinity everywhere. Their ability to regard a communion wafer as holy grants them an ever-expanding awareness of the holiness of all things, and they enter into communion with the universe. For my family, it will be the latter.

There is holiness in all things. There exists the universal within the particular, and the particular within the universal. And insofar as God is Love, I believe in God with my whole being. So, my family and I go each Sunday to join hands and sing praises to Love. The Eucharist is not a secret ritual where I encounter the divine for a single moment, but a joyous celebration of the divine that I encounter in all things at all moments.

There is value in creating myths that need deconstructing. There's value in giving a child the security of a small worldview, while also giving them the tools to climb out of it when they are ready. And in the reconstruction, there are vital truths found in the rubble.

In spite of all the self-avowed Catholics and Christians who use their faith as justification for individualism, violence, and hatred, I believe that Catholicism is truly an antidote for those things — or at least it should be. There is no bearded white man in the sky, there is no burning pit promising eternal torture, there is no magic spell that a select few can cast to absolve you of your sins. I do not know what happens after we die. I do not know the historicity of the Gospels. I do not know how the universe came into being. But I don't think it actually matters.

Of course, I'm supremely biased. I'm coming from an experience where the Church granted me safety in a time of pain. It is what I know, and it's what I know how to give others.

I look deep within myself, past all appearance, label, experience, programming, and memory, and I see something infinite. It's something eternal. Theologian Richard Rohr calls it 'The Immortal Diamond'. And then I look out beyond the universe, past the edges of time and space, and I see the same thing. So if that infinity exists both within and without, then what am I other than connected to all things? What is the universe other than a singularity with billions of parts that merely appear to be separate? What is existence other than relationship? When a raindrop is birthed from the cloud, it believes with all its being that it is separate and distinct from every other raindrop, until it reaches the ocean.

So, I'll give my child the gift of ancient tradition. I'll give my child a community of like-minded Christians who seek to better the world, and move the Church in new directions. And then when ready, I'll be there for the deconstruction. I'll be there to help carve paths from belief into Truth.

26

SUPREMELY SELF-AWARE

Living, it seems, has a number of perplexing side effects.

In September of 2022, I was reeling. I was almost 32 years old, had errantly achieved niche online infamy, spent two years burning myself out on a fundraising mission, was the target of malicious attacks from within that company that triggered repressed experiences of childhood scapegoating, met and subsequently went no-contact with my biological father, and I was unemployed. I grew suspicious of my friends, projecting the hurt and betrayal of the last two years onto them. I grew distant from Natalie, too. Our life together had become about things crashing around us, me holding her down to inject her with hormones, and her own mental anguish regarding her body's lack of cooperation. And I was angry with myself. My own journey of fatherhood was about to begin, and I was at the lowest point in my mental health since I first left home.

I was angry. This isn't the way I wanted things to go. I wanted to be at the top of my game. I had scraped and labored and fought to be the best parent possible. I read, researched, planned, and built systems and spreadsheets about parenting, but I hadn't taken care of my own mental health. My entire life was an arc towards fatherhood, and here I was crashing and burning right before it began.

But spring doesn't ask winter's permission, and choosing to allow growth needs none either.

I started therapy.

In my twenties I developed quite a lot of coping mechanisms. I'm not sure if they'd be labeled as healthy or unhealthy, but they were adaptive. They allowed me to step out of the annihilation of self-hatred for a time, and build the life I wanted.

I had a perception of being defined by paradoxes. A sense of polar opposites being true, and having to juggle impossibilities. I had a narrative of needing to perform the role of the hero, to conceal that I was a villain. I didn't feel permitted to merely be a 'person'. I wasn't allowed to have flaws, or desires. I had to do everything for everyone, and if I failed, I wasn't merely a human who made mistakes: I was a cancer that my loved ones would quickly excise. I was tormented by recurring nightmares: a house fire, an apocalypse, or a war zone where I had to get everyone to safety.

In my twenties, I developed a personal myth of self – an idea of who I was that protected me. In this myth, I didn't care about aesthetics, or presentation. I didn't care about my own health or comfort. I was above those superficial things. I felt most alive when I was creating an enjoyable experience for someone else. In this myth, I had conquered emotion. I looked down at anyone who let their emotions be in control, and felt superior. I believed I had achieved total self control. I could suppress any feeling and articulate a logical explanation for anything I chose to do, and I called it enlightenment.

Meanwhile, I desperately needed to prove my value to everyone. I needed to demonstrate constantly that I was worth spending time with, because you would benefit from my intelligence, creativity, compassion, or planning. In fact, I had to earn my entire existence. I was born out of sin, after all. My protector-self was always telling my child-self, "Be prepared for everyone to hate you. They'll see you as a monster, so you have to convince them that the monster is a useful one to keep around."

In my early twenties, complex post-traumatic stress disorder (CPTSD) was often in the driver's seat. I would insist on sitting with my back to the wall in any open area, refusing to allow people to be behind me. I harbored resentment towards anyone older than me, predicting that they'd use their implicit authority to hurt me. I had a need to be in control of everything. As the most prominent effects of the CPTSD receded, it settled into mere repression of all feelings – especially anger. I repressed anger, because I believed that anger inevitably became violence, and violence became shame.

Those emotions would certainly leak out in various ways in my life. As a teenager, it was rage at my mother, as I leaned into the role of being the 'cause' of division in the family. Then, it was codependency on Natalie and relying on her to be the ever-sustaining source of affirmation and reassurance. Then it was obsessively curating every experience for my friends so I was appreciated and indispensable. Then it became shaming myself for a lack of success, and a failure to provide my family with everything they deserved.

And now, in my thirties, the coping mechanisms that fueled me a decade ago were suddenly insufficient. I needed new ones.

And at first, I was unsure I even needed therapy. After all, I regarded myself as supremely self-aware, and unafraid to examine any aspect of my history. I would freely tell stories of my childhood to anyone who was interested, and I demanded careful introspection from both myself and others. But with that commitment to self-knowledge came an inherent ignorance of the parts of myself that had been left behind. The part of myself that was still in that bedroom, being hit by my dad. The part of myself still looking up into my mother's eyes, waiting for a sign that she knew what was happening was wrong. And the part of me that had moved on and could regard his past unemotionally, hated the part of me that was still back there.

I have always believed deeply in the value and importance of gaining agency over your emotions. I clung to the idea that you can simply choose to be happy. I scorned people who complained of being made to feel angry or sad, or who dodged responsibility for their actions as if they were inevitable results of their feelings. I insisted that if you are scared, or sad, or furious, you are on some level allowing that to occur, and are responsible for it. And, in many ways I still believe there is a nugget of truth in that. But I didn't understand the extent I was hiding behind that conviction. I didn't understand that gaining that agency in a healthy way requires a huge amount of self care, integration and awareness – not merely suppressing all feeling in order to claim that agency.

I started tracking my emotions, and checking in with my body. I kept a chart of my mood and mental wellbeing for two years, trying to illustrate my mental health with data and find correlations. As I stayed present to myself, I noticed a strange pattern: I would have bouts of high productivity and creativity that came with a sense of ease and peace. Then, that would crash into deep anxiety, where I'd find myself unable to do anything but lay about and ruminate about what lurked around every corner.

In the highs, I'd be able to take creative risks, willing to start a new job or write a story. In the lows, I'd need the comfort of something mathematical and predictable, like a programming project – or, too often, a video game. In the highs, I'd seek out new social connections and novel experiences. In the lows, I'd retreat to my closest friends and search for their affirmation that I was accepted. It was like a personality shift that cycled back and forth, and I hated myself for it each time. I started remembering this pattern occurring again and again – working at the university, for example, I'd be an incredibly high performer, doing three times the expected output of my job, until I would suddenly switch off. Then I'd start arriving late and leaving early, coasting on my reputation as a high performer and obscuring my lack of output. Then suddenly, I'd find the composure and energy to start creating again. The same thing happened in all eras of my life, like a sine wave in a cord that had been snapped in that first hibernation period in college, traveling forward through time.

I started mapping this out, looking back at that mood data and past projects to create a calendar of these peaks and valleys. I looked at when I last opened a file to write a poem, or when I binged a certain video game. The pattern came into sharp focus: 78 days. At 78 days, on the day, a switch would flip in my mind and I'd wake up in a thick fog, ruminating about the terrors of the world. It's like I was sucked back into the past, and my mind was in survival mode. Then 78 days later I'd wake up in the present, willing and able to enumerate my goals and work towards them.

This was beyond bizarre. If anyone else had told me this, I wouldn't believe them. And I'd certainly warn them against creating a self-fulfilling prophecy. Still, I monitored this with my therapist, and practiced reparenting myself through it. During the highs, I allowed myself to pursue my goals while still reminding myself to take time to rest without burning out. During the lows, I worked on not shaming myself for simply resting. The switchovers came on cue, every 78 days.

I was diagnosed with a form of Cyclothymia. At least, that is the most useful term we could find for it. It is a mood disorder, characterized by cyclic shifts between hypomanic and depressive – milder and more gradual than bipolar disorder. Still, the 78 day period is more than unusual. I researched as much as I could – does 78 days correlate to any internal biological clock? Is it seasonal? Is it astronomical? Is it my gut health, my sleep schedule, my endocrinology? But, nothing. No one has ever reported a consistent periodicity like this, and 78 days is not a cycle found anywhere else. It just doesn't make sense. My own personal Groundhog Day.

27

THE UNKNOWN IS NOT THE DARK

I 've always been of two minds about hope. I cling to it and run from it in equal measure, trying to juggle the benefits that come from venturing forward with the risks that lurk within the unknown.

For as long as I can remember, it's felt like my job is to protect everyone I care about. This is a role that was foisted upon me in many ways, but also has been a job I've continued to carry out long after anyone asked me to.

There are a lot of deeply layered reasons that I perceive myself in this role. Much of it has to do with being parentified at a young age, and scapegoated for the choices of others. Some of it has to do with internalizing the idea that my only value comes from what I provide to those around me. There's also the confusing, swirling, blinding artifices of gender - as a man, I should be protecting, providing, stewarding, and safeguarding, right?

But suffice it to say that the 'unknown' has been the singular most fearsome boogey-man in my life. My frame of reference tells me that engaging with the unknown is like driving a car in the dark, with no headlights. I could easily hit a tree, or career off a cliff, and cause great injury to myself and my passengers. What a fool I would be, to get in that car.

Much of my cognitive energy throughout my life is devoted to the process of predicting the future. If I can just collect enough data, and anticipate enough of other people's choices, I can prepare for any eventuality. This is not an unusual experience for those who come from a household with a narcissistic and abusive parent. In fact, many people who live for years in a toxic system report having an uncanny sense of intuition, ESP, or prediction. This is because their brain, in a constant background process that they may or may not be aware of, is constantly trying to analyze and predict everything. This is a normal coping mechanism, but one that causes significant drain.

Yet, I want to engage more in creative pursuits. There's an urge to take chances, and put myself out there in a vulnerable way. But there's this voice in my head that tells me to avoid the unknown.

What if you spend a month working on a short story, and it ends up being bad? That's a month wasted. A month that could have instead been spent on taking care of the people who rely on you, you selfish bastard. A month that could have been spent figuring out how to write better. Or better yet, spent grinding to fill your son's college fund with a more dependable income stream. You should have just spent more time planning, analyzing, and collecting enough data to know either how to actually write that story well, or you shouldn't have written it at all. You got in the car, in the dark, with no headlights, hoping for the best, but you careened off a cliff and now all of your passengers are that much less well off. Avoid the unknown!

Damn.

As I become more aware of this imprisoning logic, I've been turning it over and over in my head trying to figure out exactly how it's been twisted into something harmful. Because, on the face of it, it just seems *right*. Engaging in an artistic pursuit, or taking risks, IS the unknown. And with the unknown, comes the risk of failure. it even bears the risk of ending up in a worse place than you started. It certainly carries the opportunity cost of what you could have spent resources on instead.

And there are people in my life that rely on me. My wife and my child at the very least. My choices affect them. I have a duty to be as responsible as possible, right? I can't just get in the car, in the dark, with no headlights, and expect to keep them safe.

But... resilience, adaptability, and exploration are valuable. Risk-taking is part of life, and should be handled with care, not avoided entirely. A balance can be struck, can't it?

But that just doesn't feel right. I can't get my mind to accept the idea that there's any level of tolerable threat to those I care about.

So what's happening here? What is the growth opportunity?

Let's frame this as a maladaptive belief:

If I engage with the unknown, I could waste my time and cause injury to the safety of those I have under my care. Therefore, I should never engage with the unknown because it is wrong to risk the safety of those I care about. As a father, spending my time on the unknown is like driving a car with my eyes closed. It's irresponsible and risks the safety of my passengers. If I engage in a creative project without knowing the outcome, it could be a waste of time and injure the economic safety of my family.

Hmm... what's wrong with this? I thought of a few things.

Perhaps, the answer is just to have hope! Hope cures all!

I value hope a lot, but no, this is not it. I can't just drive that car in the total dark, and rely on mere hope that I won't bring injury to those in the car with me.

Perhaps, the trees and cliffs don't exist! You can drive in the dark and you'll be safe!

Er, no. Engaging with the unknown carries risk. That's just a fact.

But then, I had a realization.

This maladaptive belief has been forged over 30 years of shame and self-denial. And at its core, the ultimate lie, is that I am not capable. That I'm not able to accomplish what needs to be done, so I must rely on this unachievable goal of perfect, complete information about my environment. Otherwise, it feels like I am blind.

And there's the truth, revealing itself.

The Unknown Is Not The Dark.

That truth eluded me for so long, because it just feels true that any amount of unknown is total blindness. And if that premise is true, then the rest of my logic completely makes sense.

But what's actually true, is that engaging with the unknown is not operating in the dark, and I have every capacity to maintain safety even though I don't know exactly where I'm headed. If the destination is unknown, that doesn't mean I'm driving in the dark. I still have my wits, I can see the road just fine, and I'm capable enough to adapt to any twists in the path. I might not end up where I expect, but everyone will still be safe, and I can detour or change routes as needed.

I'm capable. The unknown is certainly unknown, and can be terrifying. But the unknown is not the dark.

28

INTEGRATION

I worked through the anger. I deconstructed these myths of self, and reconnected with my child self. In all my efforts to become the ultimate parent, I was finally realizing that first I needed to reparent myself. And then, I remembered that visualization exercise that yanked me out of that deep pit in college, years ago: Alternate Universe Alex. I needed to develop a picture of the man I want to be.

The man I want to be feels his emotions freely. He has a strong memory but forgives easily. He allows space for his own needs, and takes time to rest. He celebrates the work and the journey that brought him to an accomplishment just as much as the accomplishment, because they are one and the same.

He eats well, he listens to his body, and he keeps himself clean. He takes time to create an environment that fosters a positive headspace. He is intentional about parenting himself with compassion, and reminds himself that he has worth. He creates something for future generations to treasure, and ignores those who judge it as inferior. He knows that urgency is rarely needed. He is expansive, and takes up space.

He makes time to tell others what they mean to him. He shares his positive attitude with them as it overflows, and gives to himself the same approach and care he gives to others. He knows that he owes himself patience and gentleness.

He breathes deeply, drinks water, eats slowly, moves often, and seeks purpose. He is grateful.

It's funny. One of the most common refrains of my dad's abuse was an insistence on gratitude.

Beating me with a paddle on my back, saying, "you should be grateful you're not bleeding. It could be worse."

Slapping me in the face, saying, "you should be grateful you're even allowed to live here. It could be worse."

Throwing me through walls, saying, "you should be grateful I don't kill you. It could be worse."

That idea stuck inside me, and infuriated me. I rebelled against the concept of gratitude, because of how twisted it was served to me. Gratitude seemed useless. Gratitude was excusing pain and harm merely because it could be worse. Gratitude was accepting stagnation and refusing to improve. Gratitude was self-congratulatory and selfish. Gratitude gave people permission to hurt you.

When I finally picked up my anger, and looked at it closely, I winced, expecting to see imprisoning rage. I expected to see a fury that would be all-consuming. Instead, I saw gratitude. Gratitude for the Gorslines who raised me for my first three years of life, impressing upon me a formative seed of belongingness. Gratitude for my uncles who gave me their time and mentorship. For my granddad, who, for all of his faults, simply gave me space to be a kid. For the community at my childhood church who created another nexus of belongingness just as I was about to unravel. For Natalie, who saw me as worthy of her time even when I was a filthy agoraphobe. For the privilege of being both white and male in the face of abuse and poverty. For my siblings, who grew out of that toxic environment and are willing to see me as a friend, and not a scapegoat or agitator. For my friends, a community of love and support. And for my mother, who in all of her complicity and denial bestowed upon me a love of adventure, magic, and family.

Over the years I had many different conceptions of what healing might mean. I thought it meant disconnecting from the past, so it can't affect me. I thought it meant forgiving those who harmed me, somehow absolving them of their cruelty. I thought it meant assembling my identity into labels, or deconstructing it into cause-effect chains across the years. I thought it meant building a life that perpetually filled all the needs left by a wanting childhood.

Instead, healing meant deconstructing the toxic form of gratitude I had been taught. It meant allowing myself to be grateful for all the incredible people and places that gave me kindness, without feeling like that was saying that the abuse was okay.

I deserved better, and I am grateful.

29

GRATITUDE

I am finishing this memoir at the end of my 33rd year on Earth. I am doing some freelancing work and writing for small businesses. My gamble on Bitcoin over a decade ago did not blossom into obscene riches, but I am grateful to draw from it now as a small financial cushion. I am privileged to have just enough savings to work freelance jobs from home, pursue therapy, be immersed in the first crucial years of my son's life, prepare for our second child's birth, and write this memoir.

As I write these final words of this memoir, there is a not-so-small amount of panic. My brain is swirling with a paralyzing cacophony of voices that urge me to stuff this book into a box and burn it. *This is too vulnerable to publish! You're laying your entire childhood bare for the world to see — have you no shame? Your writing ability is on display, too, and the world will find it wanting. One day, you won't want your life to be remembered this way, and you won't be able to take it back. Do you really think your great-grandchildren will benefit from this sob story? Don't you think it will suck to have your trauma enshrined on strangers' shelves? Even worse, on your friends' shelves? You're offering up all your memories and experiences to be rated on a five-star scale by people who couldn't care less about what you've been through. Oh, you think this is art? This is merely the ramblings of a silly man. Don't delude yourself. Even this paragraph is a thinly-veiled attempt at deflecting imagined criticism.*

I take a deep breath. I remember the gratitude that brought me to this place of owning my story. And I feel that the final step in owning it is to publish it. They say to write what you know. In a way, I feel that the contents of this book are all I've ever known — and I'd like to finally start knowing something else.

My journey into fatherhood has been my journey into gratitude. It's been the growing realization that I'm not the hero of my story. My wife, Natalie, is the hero of this story, and she always has been. And now I'm no longer the main character – and I don't want to be.

If my experiences thus far have taught me anything, it's this: if you lie down with dogs, you get up with fleas. But you get up anyhow, and say thank you to the world for the privilege of being awake.